I Love This Place

Amplify Your School Culture to Reignite Staff, Reconnect Students, and Rally Community

Patrick M Erwin

First Paperback and Hardback Edition

PB ISBN: 978-1-7369001-6-1
HB ISBN: 978-1-7369001-7-8
E-book ISBN: 978-1-7369001-8-5

Printed in the United States of America

To Aaren, for leading me well.

"I Love Our Place"

Contents

Foreword

I HAVE TO admit something to you. Each year, I fight the temptation to chuckle when I meet a recent graduate who tells me they plan to immediately begin their own business as a consultant. I don't say this because I have no faith in young job seekers. I genuinely do. I'm tempted to chuckle because I am looking at a young person with classroom experience but no career experience who now wants to counsel an executive or entrepreneur who's been on the job a while. Even if the graduate's classroom experience was extraordinary, it likely was made up from lectures and discussions in a safe environment, not on-the-job training. The stakes were low. That young graduate may have great theories, but they're theories. It's like getting marriage advice from a single person or parenting advice from someone with no kids. Experience just makes the advice-giver wiser. Someone once said, "Before I was married, I had seven theories on raising children. Now I have seven children and no theories." That's often how life feels. Gaining years of experience just keeps things real. Someone who's done something over and over usually has deeper levels of empathy, better insights and usually comes across as authentic in their counsel.

That's what you'll find in this book.

Patrick Erwin's ideas in this book are borne from seventeen years of experience in a school classroom and in leading the marching band at Hillgrove High School in Cobb County, just north of Atlanta. On top of that, he's served several more years at our non-profit, Growing Leaders, where he gets to observe and collaborate with K-12 schools. He not only provides wise counsel in this book, but you'll quickly see he understands the nuances of a classroom, the subtle factors that influence a school culture, and provides steps that are both transferable (anyone can practice them) and transformational (they will change your school atmosphere) that you can implement on your campus. The ideas are straightforward and achievable for anyone.

What I love most about Patrick and this book is that the lessons he shares often stem from his failures. And he's up front about that. He communicates how he had to overcome his own arrogance and build his self-awareness as an educator. He shares how he learned to listen to students, not just instruct students, which was hard when he knew he was paid to teach, not listen. In short, the work of creating a great culture began with recreating himself. In this book, you'll discover his assumptions about leadership and teaching, some of which proved to be spot on and others that proved to be wrong. He's up front about both.

At the heart of the book, he reveals a framework he found useful as he attempted to impact the culture of his students and to ultimately influence his school culture. The ingredients in his recipe spell the word: HUSTLE. Each one challenges you to begin with an inward commitment to embody a quality in yourself, like humility, understanding, scholarship, trust, leadership, and excellence, then demonstrate it to colleagues and students. In short, school culture is transformed when we practice what we preach. Like Patrick, we must learn it, then do it, then share it. In the words of John Maxwell, good leaders know the way, go the way, then show the way. Anything short of this is hollow, artificial and temporary.

Over the last several years, I have known Patrick as an educational partner as he taught at Hillgrove High School, then later as a colleague when we invited him to join our team at Growing Leaders. We hired him because we'd seen him embody the very qualities we wanted to see in educators everywhere. As you read this book, you'll enjoy his sense of humor, his genuine spirit, and his practical counsel, especially if you're an educator. But I want to challenge you—you'd better be ready to put into practice what he talks about. It's only in applying what we know that changes us and those around us. Information without application leads to stagnation.

I recall launching Growing Leaders in 2003. My goal was to cultivate leadership in young people wherever we could find them—on a school campus, on a sports team, at a workplace, in a non-profit or in a youth group. When we found Patrick and his wife Aaren, I knew we had found kindred spirits who were about the very same goal. He was using Habitudes® (which is now combined with John Maxwell's principles and called iLead) to build not just good students and musicians, but good leaders. And many of his students came to say the words he chose to use as the title of his book, *I Love This Place.*

May that be your story as well.

Tim Elmore
Founder of Growing Leaders
TimElmore.com

1

Techniques and Strategy Are Not Enough

SINCE I WAS in college, there have been two things I have always wanted to achieve. First, I always wanted to be the head band director at a High School in Cobb County, Georgia, one of the country's top 150 communities for music.

Second, I wanted to begin a book in the nerdiest possible way.

Boom. Mission accomplished.

In 2006, I was lucky enough to be chosen to help open a brand-new high school in the county mentioned above. It was one of the greatest and most challenging honors of my professional career. In my second year of teaching, I landed a dream job.

I spent sixteen years at that school. During my time there, we averaged an enrollment of 316 students, with around twice that many parents/guardians, a staff of about a dozen, and a nearly $300,000 booster club budget. It was a miniature machine—a microcosm of a school. I learned a lot about leading an organization in those years. In fact, the only difference between my job and my principal's job was scale.

But in 2007, as a twenty-six-year-old new teacher, all I had was confidence. I was 100 percent certain that I had all the answers already. Of course, my students loved me because I was young and fun. Of course, I was doing an excellent job teaching them. Of course, things were great! One day, in search of validation of my greatness, I wandered over to the website Rate-My-Teacher.com. It is a since-defunct site where students could anonymously give their teachers ratings at the time. What could go wrong?

For me, nothing! I knew they loved me. So, I popped open a search window and typed in my school, finding my name near the top. A fresh rating!

It read:

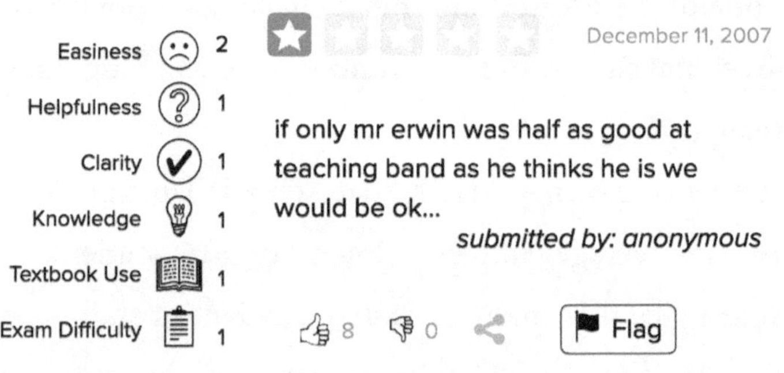

OUCH! It seems that my boorish confidence wasn't fooling any of my students. I'm sure my colleagues at the time would agree.

I wish I could say that moment brought about an instant life change, but it didn't. I did make several changes, though. I decided I needed more skills and resources. Over the next several years, I got another degree. I learned new pedagogical strategies and integrated new technology (the first-generation iPad wasn't cheap, but we had one!). I also tried new classroom management approaches. And I improved. I got better as a teacher.

But something was still missing. I was making a key mistake that teachers and school leaders often make. I assumed that getting better at my job would create a great culture for my classes and our organization. Unfortunately, that's only partially true. I had to learn the value of growing leaders.

In the spring of 2018, I realized that what I had been focusing on was not enough. We had just gathered our recruiting data for the following year: the number of eighth graders coming to the high school band as freshmen. For years, we had averaged around 120 incoming members. That year, the number was eighty-two. Houston, we had a problem!

Later, I asked my wife what she thought. She's also a high school teacher and one of the wisest people I know. She set me straight, saying:

"I can't help but notice something about you.
You preach a lot of leadership to your students,
but don't seem to practice a lot of leadership for yourself."

That hurt. But she was right. I had been focusing on the wrong things when it came to building a culture that students wanted to be a part of. Just being good at my job was not enough. My students needed a leader who cared about them. They needed a leader who built a culture that welcomed them in. From that day on, I dedicated myself to growing leaders in my classroom and becoming a better leader myself.

Author Clint Pulver describes it this way, "Most people are willing to adapt just about anything about the way they conduct business, except for their style of leadership."[1]

The changes that occurred in me personally were incredible as I leaned into changing my leadership style to meet the needs of the people around me. Before, I thought I was charismatic, but I was just gregarious. Being loud gets you noticed, but that's not the same as charisma or likeability.

As I began to change myself, I noticed students came to me more with their thoughts and ideas. My colleagues and I got along better. I became the department chair of fine arts. My relationship with my wife and kids improved. I became more approachable to those around me.

The day of real validation for me came when the school front office clerk, Mrs. Morgan, stopped me in the hallway. She looked me in the eye and said, "Mr. Erwin, you've made a pretty big life change, haven't you? I can see it. You're glowing."

It was just after this that I heard a truth that should ring in every school leader and teacher's ears:

How you do anything is how you do everything.

Adapting our pedagogy and classroom management styles is not enough. To set a culture where everyone thinks and feels, "I LOVE THIS PLACE," we must become better leaders. This is because leadership is not something we do; it is someone who we are.

GOOD NEWS BAD NEWS

Allow me to approach this point a different way. Ask yourself:

1. **Who is your favorite teacher you ever had?**
2. **Are they your favorite teacher because of what they taught, or who they are?**

In every case, I'm willing to bet it's who they are.

I had so many great teachers over the years, but one that stands out to me is Dr. Jody Butler, an elementary and middle school teacher of mine. I was in the gifted program (hair flip) and Dr Butler was our teacher. She challenged us with so many different activities and subjects from science fairs to Oregon trail. But the thing I remember most is how she treated us. Even though we were young, she treated us with the respect and care you hope every teacher gives to their students. She was tough. She was fair. And she made us feel seen, heard, and like we belonged.

While this is probably something you already know, what I really want to point out is the good news and bad news that comes along with deciding you want to be a better leader:

Good News: Your leadership matters.

Bad News: Your leadership matters DAILY.

At all times and everywhere.

Your leadership matters in the classroom, the hallway, the cafeteria, the playing field, the locker room, the faculty breakroom, the grocery store, and online. Anyone who's worked in a school knows that education is a lifestyle job. It's not just a hat you can take on and off when you're in the building. In many ways, being an educator is synonymous with being a leader. We are always being watched, scrutinized, and emulated by those we lead. It can be a hard truth but also a wonderful one. We have the power to influence those we teach and those that we lead. Our leadership matters!

It matters on good days and bad days. It matters in large groups and one-on-one. Your leadership matters whether you are standing up front with your title or sitting in the back with your friends and colleagues.

Leadership matters disproportionately to all other areas in which you can grow.

Leaders who think this way shape culture. They are the creators of movements. I believe the missing ingredient of most struggling schools is culture. I am not talking about a culture in general, but a culture centered around growing as many leaders as possible: students, teachers, staff, paraprofessionals, clerks, etc.

First, we must learn to lead ourselves. In doing so, we will determine the values, skills, habits, and attitudes we need to model to guide people to the culture we want to have in our building or classroom. The kind of culture that can impact every person in our school and the surrounding community. The type of culture where everyone looks around and can confidently say:

I LOVE THIS PLACE

THE 1-4-3

I know countless numbers of us grew up watching Mister Rogers' Neighborhood. Between that and Sesame Street, my Saturday morning was pretty much set for a decade. One of the things I remember about Fred Rogers was his love for the number 143. To Mister Rogers, 143 meant "I Love You" because it was the number of letters in each word. He celebrated the 143rd day of the year each year and even kept his weight at 143 pounds! That's commitment!

Or perhaps you had a pager when you were growing up. Anytime someone sent you the message 143, you knew they meant "I Love You."

For this book, I want to end each chapter with what I call the 1-4-3. It is a reminder that we are creating a school culture where people feel loved and share that love with others. Each of the numbers will provide you with discussion material for team meetings and transformation tables. I hope you enjoy!

THE 1-4-3 – CHAPTER 1: "TECHNIQUES AND STRATEGY AREN'T ENOUGH"

1 Quotable Quote

"How you do anything is how you do everything."

If we want students and staff to say, *"I love this place,"* then our leadership can't be limited to job descriptions or big moments. It must show up every day, everywhere.

4 Key Takeaways

1. **Leadership Over Strategy:** School culture isn't just a result of better strategies or improved teaching techniques; it emerges from intentional and visible leadership.
2. **Culture is Created, On Purpose:** Culture doesn't happen by accident. Leaders must actively shape values, habits, and attitudes to build a community where everyone feels they belong.
3. **Your Leadership Matters:** Leadership matters daily, not occasionally. From classrooms to grocery stores, teachers and school leaders are always on display and must model the values they want their culture to reflect.
4. **Start With Yourself:** The foundation of school-wide cultural transformation begins with leading

yourself—finding personal growth areas, embracing humility, and committing to being the type of leader others want to follow.

3 Questions for Your Team

1. In what ways might a shift toward intentional leadership improve our culture?
2. Think of a time when you realized your leadership style wasn't working—what changed for you, and what did you learn about yourself in that moment?
3. How can we, as a team, model daily leadership in our school environments so that students and staff begin to feel, "I love this place"?

2

The Struggle Is Real

IN THE WINTER and spring of 2020, my classes prepared for our annual large-group performance evaluation. Think of this as our state standards evaluation. The big difference between music classes and most other classes is that we take our tests as a team, on stage in front of an audience, and are judged by a jury of our peers. Sounds fun, doesn't it?

We had been having an incredible year up to this point. The bands were playing great. The students were taking the repertoire they had been given very seriously. I had given them a huge challenge that semester: the Finale to Dmitri Shostakovich's *Symphony No. 5*. It's thirteen minutes of pure EPIC "superhero soundtrack" awesomeness. We were grinding. And we were loving it.

We had just been visited by my friend Mr. Gary Speck, longtime director at Miami University (OH). Mr. Speck spent two gruelingly wonderful days with the band and had taken them to the next level of excellence. The week after he left us in early March was some of the best music-making I'd ever experienced.

Then, Friday, March 13th happened. (The universe can be cruel, but it also has a sense of humor… Friday the 13th.) Amidst the rumors of a global pandemic, we were told they were closing the schools for two weeks for a thorough cleaning. I looked at my students and told them, "We will play this music again as soon as we return." Instead of playing that Friday, we chose to talk. I recognized that they needed me to make them feel like everything would be okay, and that's what I did. They needed leadership. Not strategy and techniques.

I probably don't have to tell you—we never played that music again. We didn't come back for months.

The following school year started even worse. We didn't see a student in person until November. The year progressed slowly. It improved over time, and we eventually returned to "normal" classes the following year. But if you're like me, you've asked yourself, "What is normal?"

During that strange time between 2020 and 2022, I saw so many innovative colleagues doing amazing things! We had virtual play performances and uniquely formatted sports practices. In addition, we **didn't** have state-mandated tests. My fellow teachers were creative and free. I spoke to many colleagues who said they enjoyed teaching during the pandemic because they got to teach things that they felt mattered and didn't feel the pressure of test scores and metrics.

Of course, we had colleagues on the other side of that coin as well. I saw teachers simply giving up: "This is too hard," "There is too much technology," and "This isn't what I signed up for." A clear dividing line was drawn between the "creative innovators" and the "overwhelmed and stuck."

I've always found that during times of struggle, when we are somewhere between "I can do this" and "I give up," it's helpful to me to remember the phrase: **My Response is My Responsibility.** One key component of building an "I Love This Place" culture is for the leaders to remember what they can control: their response to situations.

MY RESPONSE IS MY RESPONSIBILITY

A truly life-giving leader knows that we can always control our attitude, thoughts, feelings, habits, work ethic, and level of positivity toward those we lead. This is not to say it will be easy, but it is necessary.

Frustration often results from trying to control things we cannot. Things like the weather, pandemics, traffic, tweets from celebrities or politicians, the number of emails we get from parents or colleagues, and more… We will never be able to control these things, and frustration will be the only result when we try.

What lies between what I can control and what I cannot control are things I can influence. John Maxwell reminds us that "leadership is influence—nothing more, nothing less." Those who struggle with influence and control will struggle as leaders.

If great culture arises from great leadership, then we must respond well and make wise decisions as often as possible. Great leaders use their influence to set the stage for the people they are leading to succeed. If you want to change the culture, start with yourself. You're the leader in charge of the school, the team, the classroom, the cafeteria, etc.

I LOVE THIS PLACE

This book's title came from an image shared on Facebook one day by a friend and fellow teacher, Katie. She had been given a new classroom in a new building. The room that she and her students were leaving behind was quite old. You know old classrooms by their smell and feel, right? They are just full of memories.

Katie had the brilliant idea to have her students write messages on the wall with permanent markers. It was their "goodbye room" activity. It was a brilliant way to end an era with some closure for all. One student wrote, "I Love This Place" on a cinder block in the middle of the room.

When I saw it, I thought "THAT'S IT!" That is the exact phrase I want every leader, teacher, and student to feel: **I Love This Place!** Not because the cinder blocks are loveable by any means. But because of what we've seen, felt, heart, and experienced inside the walls. That's the essence of great culture.

Every school leader can create an I LOVE THIS PLACE culture in their building or classroom. If we can find and define the heart of our leadership, we can share that with everyone else.

Let's start by defining school culture.

SCHOOL CULTURE

School culture has been defined in many ways by many different sources. My favorite definition comes from Michael Fullan:

> ***School culture refers to all the values, attitudes, and expected behaviors that impact a school's daily operations.***[2]

You find your culture when you consider your school and what you value in the education you provide, what attitudes you expect from the people in your building, and what behaviors you expect from them. A helpful starting exercise would be to ask these questions of yourself and your team:

1. What are the core values of our school?
2. Do we have a mission statement that our people know?
3. How would you describe the attitudes of your school employees, coworkers, and students?
4. What about the attitude your community has toward the school?
5. What are the expected behaviors of your coworkers or school employees? Students?

Answering those questions will help you define your school culture and share it with others. Culture will happen by accident if you don't create it on purpose.

Allow me to share with you three truths about school culture. First, unhappy people will complain about the **leaders** in the building. Second, happy people will get excited about the **culture**. Third, people will stay or leave, engage or tune out, persevere, or give up based on the combined influence of leadership and culture.

The first truth is one we all understand. I'm sure you've heard, or perhaps even said, things like "My principal doesn't get it," "My admin doesn't understand," "Our leaders are never even around," or even "I'm looking for other jobs, I hate this place." It seems a somewhat human truth that when things aren't going well, we look to blame our leadership.

In my teaching career, I was blessed with four great principals. Each was a great leader, but that never stopped me from complaining about them if there was a problem. Great leaders take a little bit less credit than they deserve and a little bit more blame. Unhappy people complain about their leaders most often, even when they may not deserve it.

Happy people, however, might compliment their leaders, but they will more likely comment on how they feel at school. When we feel seen, cared about, and challenged to grow, we are likelier to say, "I Love This Place."

Finally, whether people are willing to engage or tune out, choose to keep going or give up, or even decide to stay or leave for a new job, depends on both leadership and culture.

In short, culture is a really big deal.

Bamboo HR recently surveyed employees at various workplaces, and 94 percent of respondents agreed that culture is directly related to an organization's success. But is that also true for teachers?

WHAT CULTURE DO TEACHERS WANT?

In a pair of recent studies by SchoolCEO, teachers were asked what they are looking for in a job. These studies were the largest of their kind and surveyed thousands of teachers from all fifty states in 300 randomly selected school districts. The results spanned age groups and educational levels (K-12, public and private). Over 50 percent of respondents had at least a master's degree.

Notably, 79 percent of the teachers who responded belong to Generations X and Y. Most young people in teaching are from Generation Y, or, as you likely know them, Millennials (born 1983-2000). In late 2019, US Census data confirmed that Millennials had officially passed Baby Boomers as the largest living and working generation. The National Center for Education Statistics also says teachers' average age is forty-two, right on the cusp of the Gen X and Millennial generations.

The survey asked teachers about their job satisfaction and what they were most looking for to stay in the classroom. The statistics are fascinating.

Of the teachers surveyed, 65 percent reported having browsed other job opportunities within the last year. However, only 23 percent reported having applied to another job opportunity. BBC Worklife calls this "The Great Flirtation." It's a "constantly wandering eye to other openings, regardless of how long a worker has been in a role and how content they are in their job."[3]

The most interesting data I found in the survey is what those teachers consider most valuable in looking for or staying in a job. Here are the eight items they listed, ranked in order of importance:

1. Geographical Location
2. School Culture
3. School Leadership
4. Flexibility in Curriculum and Teaching
5. School Size
6. Student Performance
7. Advancement Opportunities
8. Mentorship Programs[4]

I will skip Geographical Location, although there is some wisdom in marketing your location well to potential new hires or transfers. Convincing someone to move or to commute a long way can be a tough sell.

Items 2 and 3 (ranked very closely to the first) are the easiest to control and talk about. **The largest population of**

our teaching workforce, those who will define and shape the school, really cares about school culture and leadership.

Support, respect, and appreciation were common themes in their responses. One respondent recommended building "a positive school culture with supportive administration who values educators as professionals."[5]

Another respondent said, "If a teacher knows they are supported and backed, that goes a long way in feeling happy in their job. Good teachers want to work for districts whose [leaders] have their backs and aren't just looking over their shoulders, who can help them grow without cutting them down to size."[6]

In fact, I believe these statements are true for everyone in the building: students, teachers, and other professionals. I would sum them up by saying:

"I LOVE THIS PLACE" MEANS "THIS PLACE LOVES ME."

The greatest culture we can create is one in which everyone feels seen, heard, valued, and challenged. This is a culture where students and teachers alike feel like they belong but also know they can grow. After all, it's not enough just to fit in. We want our jobs and our education system to help us build a brighter future for ourselves and our families. If I know my colleagues care about me but also have my growth in mind. I will love that place.

I recently had a conversation with a friend named Andy. He is a retired principal, having served in education for over thirty years. During our conversation, he said he thinks a principal should take (or be given) at least five to eight years before moving to another job or being reassigned by their central office. His point is that in your first three years, you're working on buy-in, getting the right people hired, moved, or even reassigned. You're establishing your norms, expectations, and values. He said it's not until at least year four or five that the school starts to feel like your own place. In that conversation, I realized that there is another reality of culture that we must keep in mind.

Culture Takes Time

One of Murphy's laws (not the one about things going wrong) is that "everything takes longer than you think it will, particularly if you're dealing with others." It's a simple fact that going anywhere with others requires more patience than going alone. This is true of family trips, group projects, team meetings, and culture building.

In a pair of recent studies on school culture, it was found that "changing the culture of a school is not an easy task. Usually, the well-intentioned values and deeply rooted perceptions of adults in the education system are firmly embedded and thus deemed sacred. Hence, cultural change is a long process, between 3-5 years."[7]

Have you ever felt like we do things in our schools simply because "that's how we've always done it?" I know I experienced that often. In education, we often become calloused about change. There's always a new initiative, government mandate, or new-fangled pedagogical idea that seems to fizzle out in about three to five years, isn't there?

However, many teachers also bring deeply rooted, firmly embedded, and even SACRED values and perceptions to their jobs. Change is hard when it comes from outside the school building and even harder when it comes from within.

Do you believe there some things that could stand to change? What do you love about your place, versus what would you change about it? What if we created culture with a three-to-five-year plan in mind?

Let's pause here and consider some questions:

1. How do you typically react to change?
2. What words, thoughts, and feelings do you want to be used to describe your school three to five years from now?
3. What needs to change in order to make those things a reality?

CAPTURING THE HEART OF YOUR SCHOOL CULTURE

Three to five years is a long time. However, as a wise person once told me, if the only thing stopping you from pursuing something great is the time it will take, start today. The following may help get you started.

In a 2022 study by the non-profit Adopt a Classroom, over 4,000 K-12 educators were surveyed. In that study, one statistic stood out to me:

> **98 percent of teachers surveyed said they feel undervalued by society and their community.** [8]

One teacher quoted in the data sums it up perfectly:

> *"Teachers need positive and productive support. We try to give as much as possible (financially, emotionally, physically, mentally) to help our students succeed. But sometimes – even that is not enough. The school used to be the heart of the community."*[9]

THE SCHOOL USED TO BE THE HEART OF THE COMMUNITY!

I know when I was growing up, everything revolved around school and the people inside. My parents and my friends' parents were intent on making sure that we respected our teachers and that any poor marks needed to be fixed by us.

However, over the last several years, there seems to have been a shift in how we view our schools and teachers. I have seen less respect shown for teachers' expertise and less accountability for our students. This has led to what we sometimes refer to as "Dry Cleaner Parenting". [10]

The idea of the dry cleaner is that you drop your clothes off dirty and wrinkled and pick them up clean and pressed. That's the dry cleaner's job. In a world that increasingly offers specialized services (like dry cleaning), it's easy for parents to assume that they drop their kids off at school to be "cleaned and pressed," aka to learn, grow, and graduate. If your clothes come back from the cleaners dirty or stained, it's not the clothes fault! I think you see where I'm going with this. Teachers have taken more than their share of blame for student's struggles.

I admit, this isn't the case everywhere, but our conversations at Growing Leaders over the past few years have slanted toward teachers feeling less valued and more alone.

How do we get to the heart of the community? We must make our response our responsibility, and this can only be done from the inside (both inside ourselves and within the building), with a heart toward school culture—more specifically, a culture of growing leaders.

FOSTERING A CULTURE OF LEADERSHIP GROWTH

A great school culture is centered around growing leaders. It starts with the school leaders. There is no way around the truth that the leader must be a role model when it comes to cultural transformation. I recently read, "The [leader] sets the tone, leads with inspiration, remains visible, and is the ultimate cultural rock. A [leader] who is consistent in behavior, focused on implementing new processes and practices, and is committed to creating a place where people are thriving like never before will pave the way for a new (or revived) healthy culture."[11] Talk about hitting the nail on the head.

We must discover the culture and leadership that we want, develop it in ourselves, and share it with others as intentionally as possible. With that in mind, let me introduce two big ideas that will drive all of my chapters:

1. I can add value by growing myself as a leader.
2. I can **amplify** that value by growing **others** as leaders.

Amplification is where the magic is. One of the first discoveries that a healthy leader makes is that they can't do it all themselves. Leaders who struggle with delegating often lack the confidence that others will get things done the "right way." But, when we take them time to develop others in the same way we develop our own leadership, we can cultivate teams of people with shared values, habits, attitudes, and ideas. While they may not do things the same way we do them, they can operate with the same spirit and within the same mission. That's amplification: shared leadership values and shared ownership.

Building a culture around leadership is the way to do that. We can't return the school to the heart of the community on our own. By acting as teams of leaders, we can. My friend and mentor, Dr. Tim Elmore, often says people must meet one of the following conditions to change:

1. They know enough that they can change.
2. They care enough that they want to change.
3. They hurt enough that they have to change.[12]

It took some hurting for me to change. When I looked at the organization I was building and noticed we had a culture problem, I had to adjust; developing my leadership and sharing that development with those I was leading. You see, once the conditions for change are met, the only thing missing is the tools to make it happen. Keep reading; the rest of the book contains practical tools and ideas for culture and leadership change.

THE 1-4-3 – CHAPTER 2: "THE STRUGGLE IS REAL"

1 Quotable Quote:

"My response is my responsibility."

We can't always control what's happening in our schools or the world—but we can always control how we show up in it. That's leadership.

4 Key Takeaways

1. **"My Response Is My Responsibility":** Leaders don't always choose their circumstances, but they can always choose how they respond—and that response shapes culture.
2. **Influence Over Control:** Effective leaders shift their focus from controlling external outcomes to influencing people through consistent habits and wise decision-making.
3. **Culture Should Start With the Leader:** Positive school culture grows from within; leaders who actively model clear values and expected behaviors.
4. **Struggle Often Reveals Leadership:** Difficult moments clarify who is truly leading—those who respond with vision and ownership naturally become culture builders.

3 Questions For Your Team

1. How do you usually respond to struggle? Why?
2. Have you ever seen a leader who was bent on trying to control things they could not? What was the result?
3. What values, attitudes, and behaviors are you modeling that can shape school culture?

3

The Leader They Need

HAVE YOU EVER looked in the mirror and felt that something needed to change, but you didn't know where to start? That was me in the spring of 2017. I mentioned that our program was having trouble recruiting, and I knew part of the problem was that I needed to be a better leader. I didn't know where to turn. A friend of mine recommended a book by John Maxwell called *360 Degree Leadership*. This book is a must-read for anyone who wants to grow as a leader. It helped me realize that we must learn to lead in all directions: down, sideways, and up.

Most leaders are good at leading down. As teachers, we know how to lead our students well, provide a good example, be professional, create a positive learning environment, and be willing to try new things to engage students. Downward leadership comes with the territory—it's expected and often intuitive.

Leading sideways can be challenging. You may be leading peers who have fewer years than you (or more). They may teach a different content area or have different administrative duties. You may be the principal, but you need to help lead other principals. Leadership isn't a competition. The rising tide lifts all ships.

I led sideways by being supportive, encouraging, and checking in with my peers to see if I could help them in any way. Being present and approachable is a great way to grow in influence. I often forced myself go to the cafeteria for lunch. It was easy to hole up in my classroom and get to planning after eating by myself. However, it was more important to me to be visible, supportive, and connect with my peers. Those lunch conversations were some of our best connection points during the busy days and months of the year.

Finally, we must learn to lead up. Whenever I got the chance, I invited my principal to my classroom. I wanted them to see what we were doing, give them an opportunity to interact with the students, and provide them with a space to sit, relax, and observe learning. Our principals often go to classes to solve problems or put out fires. I wanted to offer the antidote to that pattern.

One particularly meaningful moment happened when we were conducting an iLead lesson on integrity with our students. The lesson centers around the metaphor of a pop quiz and how we prepare for life's unexpected trials and tests by developing our integrity.

Our principal at the time, Mrs. Stewart, had moved to Atlanta from New Orleans after Hurricane Katrina. I invited her to participate in the lesson and share her story of that unexpected trial. She loved sharing her story, and the students loved hearing from her. It was a great leadership moment for us all and one of my finest examples of "leading up."

I say all this to remind you that the first step in changing school culture, whether through mere improvement or a wholesale reversal of norms, is to look in the mirror. Are you the type of leader your people need you to be? As a principal, are you leading your staff well? Are you approachable? Do your Assistant Principals feel their voices are heard?

You may be an Assistant Principal yourself. How are you leading your boss? What level of connection to the teachers do you have? How has the standard of excellence been set?

Teachers, what strategies do you use to lead your students? Their parents? How are you leading upward through your APs to the top?

The only way to properly impact your school's culture is to start with yourself. If you want people to say, "I LOVE THIS PLACE," you must be able to say it yourself, share it with others, and then lead them to that place. In this chapter, I want to share a big picture idea for becoming the leader that people need you to be. I hope to encapsulate this idea into an easy-to-remember phrase: **tough and tender leadership.**

TOUGH AND TENDER LEADERSHIP

It seems like a paradox, but we need tough and tender leaders. You probably identify as one or the other. I think back to the coaches and leaders I've had over the years. I have had some tough leaders who were hard on me, and I have had some tender ones who made me feel good about myself. The real, life-giving leaders who made an impact on me were a balance of both.

Every leader has some degree of toughness and tenderness. These aren't switches we turn on and off, they are dials we turn up and down. Too much of one or the other can lead to trouble. Let's look at some of the ways that each can impact our leadership. To have a little fun with this, I've provided an example of each using a character from the hit television show Abbott Elementary. I thought it was poignant that each of these leadership styles happens in a show about a school.

Low Toughness, Low Tenderness: The Invisible Leader

Undoubtedly, there are people in positions of leadership who lack toughness and tenderness. They probably didn't start this way, but time, stress, superiors' demands, or a constantly changing educational system have caused them to lose touch. They don't seem to care about their relationships. They also seem to have low standards of excellence for themselves and others.

This leadership style leads to **disengagement**. These are the leaders we typically avoid. They provide no discernible benefit to us or the school, and they drain the culture with phrases like "back in my day," "kids these days," or "nO oNe WaNtS tO wOrK aNyMoRe" (That's the sarcasm font).

I'm reminded of Mr. Johnson, the seasoned veteran custodian from Abbott Elementary. He isn't technically in a formal leadership position, but he often acts as though he's in charge. Despite his big personality, he's ineffective when it comes to taking real action or leading change. He's checked out when it comes to contributing meaningfully to the school's success, often making cynical or absurd remarks like, "I could run this place if I wanted to. But I don't want to."

High Toughness, Low Tenderness: The Drill Sergeant Leader

The drill sergeant is all about getting things done. They have standards, and they know how to achieve them (their way, of course). However, the drill sergeant leader doesn't have time for connection; they need to get results. That "touchy-feely" stuff is just a waste of time. They may even see personal-professional relationships as unprofessional.

Drill sergeant leadership leads only to **rebellion**. We see this in all walks of life: the overbearing parent whose child graduates and goes off to college and goes wild, the grizzled football coach who demands his players do things his way, or even the micromanaging boss whom we can't wait to gossip or complain about when they aren't around. Rules without relationships lead to **rebellion**.

The drill sergeant leader reminds me of Abbott principal Ava Coleman. Ava is the perfect example of the high-tough, low-tender leader. She's focused on asserting her authority and getting her way, but she has little interest in connecting with her staff or understanding their needs. Her leadership style is self-serving and often manipulative, leading to dissatisfaction and rebellion from the teachers who feel unsupported. I can hear her saying, "I'm the boss, so you can either get with it or get lost."

It's worth noting that this leadership style works in some situations, often for short periods. But people will always seek better options where they feel seen and heard. High standards may lead to results, but results will only sustain your culture for so long. Plus, when things aren't going well, the drill sergeant often doubles down on toughness. And more toughness in the face of less results only leads to more rebellion.

High Tenderness, Low Toughness: The Cotton Candy Leader

I'm sure you've had cotton candy before. It starts nicely, but in the end, you're just sticky, disappointed, and over-sugared. A little cotton candy is fine. A lot is just a mess.

The cotton candy leader values connection and people above all else. They live, laugh, and love. They're your buddy, your pal, your homeboy, your "ride or die." Of course, there's nothing innately wrong with being a friend to the people you lead. Friendships at work are essential. However, when it's time to get things done or someone needs an extra push, this leader may have already lost.

Cotton candy leadership leads to **entitlement**. They are known for making exceptions, allowing people to do whatever they want to maintain peace and connection. The cotton candy leader lives to be liked. They say things like, "It's okay," or "Try again next time." Inherently, these statements are acceptable, but when we make exceptions for the sake of being liked, ignoring the things that must get done, effective leadership is impossible.

Janine Teagues is a textbook cotton candy leader. She values relationships and is always eager to help her colleagues and students, often going above and beyond to make everyone happy. However, her focus on being liked and her reluctance to enforce rules or hold people accountable can lead to chaos and entitlement, especially when things get tough. You can hear Janine saying, "I just want everyone to be happy."

No one wants to work for a leader who cannot get things done. Eventually, they lose so much respect that they fade away, likely into the realm of the invisible leader. In a moment of overcorrection, perhaps a drill sergeant leader replaces them.

The Tough and Tender Leader

When things are going well, each of the previous three styles can work. When things are good, it's easy to ignore the invisible leader. You don't need direction. When we get a lot done and the results are apparent, the drill sergeant leader works. When you need connection, the cotton candy leader is there for you. The most effective leaders will always be the ones who find a good balance between toughness and tenderness. They're the ones we turn to when things get tough.

When watching Abbott, I'm reminded of Barbara Howard. Barbara embodies the tough and tender leadership style. She has high standards and isn't afraid to share them, but she does so with care and compassion. Barbara's experience allows her to balance both discipline and support, earning respect from her students and colleagues alike. She knows when to be strict and when to show understanding, making her a true leader in the school. One quote that she said in the show embodies this idea: "There's a time for fun, and there's a time for work. And right now, it's time for work."

Tough and tender leadership leads to **respect**. This leader is someone who cares about you and cares about doing a good job because they understand an important truth:

Caring and accountability are both forms of compassion. They are two sides of the same coin.

We all want to be heard and cared for. When I'm having a bad day or need advice, I need a leader who will listen and support me. I need someone to walk me through it. But I also need a leader who cares about my growth.

If I am struggling with pedagogy, communication, classroom management, etc., and my leader ignores that and lets me flounder, that's not helpful. Please don't ignore my faults for the sake of my feelings. Lean in and let me know what I need to do. Accountability is letting me know where I need to improve and helping me find strategies to do so. It's another form of compassion. People want to grow!

To put it simply, the tough and tender leader **leaves no one behind** because they care. But they **leave no one where they found them** because they challenge them to grow.

Think about the most extraordinary leaders you know. I think you will find that they care about both people and results. For people to say, I LOVE THIS PLACE in your building, we must become tough and tender. By doing so, we can encourage others to do the same.

FINDING BALANCE

Finding a balance of toughness and tenderness is the goal. It may help to quickly contrast the two sides so that we fully understand the difference.

Tough Leader	Tender Leader
Results Focused	Relationship Focused
Big Picture	Daily Connection
Outcomes	Inputs
Funnel of Information	Filter of Information

As you look at this list, you surely identify with one side more. But they are both essential. Let's pause here for some self-reflection. Take a moment and rate your leadership on the continuums below. Mark an X where you see your leadership landing. Are you tougher or more tender when it comes to the following:

<-->
Results Focused — Relationships Focused

<-->
Big Picture — Daily Connection

<-->
Outcomes Oriented — Inputs Oriented

A culture of "I Love This Place" comes from having leaders who balance both sides. I tend to be more tender than tough. I think it's the result of striving to recruit and retain students. I wanted to be likable enough that they would stay in the band. Of course, excellence is closely tied to recruiting and retention as well. Balance can be tough.

One thing that has helped find balance is learning the difference between funnel leadership and filter leadership. If you sometimes struggle with leading different types of people (especially the younger generation of teachers and leaders), I think you'll find this next section helpful.

ARE YOU MORE FUNNEL OR FILTER?

When I started teaching in 2006, I was privileged to work with a master teacher named Chris. Chris knew everything about teaching students, managing people, and pedagogy from the front of the classroom. We didn't have as much access to information on the internet back then as we do now, so I would sit beside or behind him and watch him teach.

I also made it my purpose to take everything off his plate I could. In service to the cause, I did most of the administration so he could do most of the teaching. This allowed me to take as many notes and soak up as much of the excellent teaching as possible. I learned so much in those early years.

For me, Chris was a funnel of information and influence. Think of how a funnel works. Big on one end, small on the other. A funnel takes a lot of information and makes it possible for one person (or thing) to receive it. All I had to do was listen, learn, watch, and copy Chris so I could one day do his job. Sound familiar?

Fast forward to 2017. Chris had been promoted to the district office, and I took his job as the head director. It was the dream job I mentioned in the first sentences of the book. I immediately had the opportunity to lead several younger colleagues and student teachers. You can guess how I tried to lead them. I wanted to be a funnel for them. It didn't work. They needed me to be a filter. A filter's job is to make sure only the bits and pieces you want to get through make it. Being a filter is not about compressing information but about prioritizing and interpreting it.

One significant difference between the emerging generations of teachers and us seasoned (the nice way to say old) folk is their access to information. They are the most educated and connected generation the world has ever seen.

Think about it. These days, when I need a recipe, I search the internet—I don't go to a cookbook. Similarly, if my car needs a repair, I go to YouTube to see if I can do it myself. Suppose I want to connect with a friend? I use Facebook or FaceTime. For me, these are learned behaviors. For our younger teammates, they are innate.

The younger people I was leading were so well-educated. And what they didn't know, they could look up. Trying to manage, teach, or grow them into a miniature version of me did not work. There were arguments, slammed doors, and hurt feelings.

In one instance, I invited an older, retired teacher to help us grow. He is a master teacher and one of the most respected in the country. His advice was not to let the younger teachers teach any classes for at least a semester. He wanted them to sit and watch me until they figured out how to teach like I did. He wanted me to be a funnel. It was textbook drill sergeant leadership. I'm proud that I did not take his advice that time.

What I had to learn the hard way was that I needed to connect with my younger colleagues to help them feel seen and known. I needed to empower them to feel like they could succeed independently and give feedback in private. It was a hard-learned lesson. In fact, I wish I could apologize to more than one of those wonderful young teachers for not figuring it out sooner.

As the older teachers and leaders in the building, we often forget that our younger colleagues aren't the same as us. The generation gap between us is more expansive than you might think. As Dr. Elmore often says, "Our veterans and rookies come from different worlds. They need to be led with different words."[13]

Dr. Elmore has helped me remember this concept, often reminding: **Our younger colleagues and students don't need us to be a funnel of information. They need us to be a filter who helps with interpretation and application.** (And maybe a bit of inspiration to boot.)

The tough and tender leader helps those they lead filter the clutter of information they already have, find what is relevant and valuable, and toss out the rest.

We should also lead students in this way. Remember, they have all the information in the world in their pockets (YouTube, TikTok, Instagram, TED Talks, etc.). Nearly anything we can teach our students can be learned on the Internet. We must act as filters for our students, helping them find the information they need to lead better lives and serve their communities.

One way we can do this is by providing opportunities for students to use their voices, converse peer-to-peer, and serve their community. Our iLead lessons always involved peer-to-peer conversation. Students need curated opportunities to speak to each other. The question could be simple, like "Who do you know that is a responsible leader?" or something deeper, like "What are one to two steps you can take to be a more responsible leader in your life?"

The think-pair-share model works great for student voice. I would pause to make them think. No one spoke for at least thirty seconds (preventing the shout-out, knee-jerk answer). After that, students talked to each other for a few minutes, which helped foster connection. Then, they shared with me, and we talked as a group.

In those group talks, I can be a filter for them. I can validate their ideas and congratulate their courage in sharing and offer my wisdom and perspective to their thoughts and ideas. This space also allows me to share my own stories, helping them see how these conversations are good for us all.

One more thing about funnels and filters: funnel leaders can be a point of failure. They must be present for progress to occur. It's a sad situation that if I'm not there, you can't grow! For our younger teammates, we can be a point of filter! Imagine a team of seasoned veteran leaders lined up to help young teachers prioritize, interpret, filter, and apply the wealth of information available. The results would be amazing!

A FRAMEWORK TO BECOME TOUGH AND TENDER

Becoming a tough and tender leader will take work, but it's not as complicated as you might think. In the following chapters, I will give you a framework of six specific and practical steps that you can take to grow as a leader. You can read them in order or just turn to the one that most interests you. Choose your adventure!

THE 1-4-3 – CHAPTER 3: "THE LEADER THEY NEED"

1 Quotable Quote

"Caring and accountability are both forms of compassion. They are two sides of the same coin."

If you only care without challenging, you create entitlement. If you only challenge without care, you breed rebellion. The sweet spot is balancing both.

4 Key Takeaways

1. **Lead in All Directions:** Healthy leadership isn't just top-down; it includes influencing peers and superiors by adding value, building connections, and taking initiative.
2. **Balance Tough and Tender:** Great leaders set high standards and build strong relationships—both are essential to gain respect.
3. **Be a Filter, Not a Funnel:** Today's students and young teachers don't need more content—they need help filtering, applying, and connecting it.
4. **Self-Awareness is the Starting Point:** Leadership improvement starts with recognizing your default style and adjusting to meet others' needs.

3 Questions for Your Team

1. Would the people you lead say you're tougher or more tender? What might they need more of from you?
2. How have you seen "funnel style" leadership play out in your career? What shifts could be made to be more of a filter for people?
3. Who in your school needs more *care* from you right now—and who needs more *accountability*?

4

Good Things Come to Those Who HUSTLE

IF YOU VISITED one of our practices in the sixteen years I led the band at Hillgrove, you would have heard **"HUSTLE"** more than any other word. It wasn't just the coaches yelling at the students to move faster; the students were yelling it themselves.

We practiced an average of eight hours a week. In those eight hours, we had to figure out how to get 180+ students to move and play the same way, at the same time, as well as they could. Marching band is a performance art. Everyone is a starter. There are no reserves.

We also "put on a show" at every Friday football game. To be frank, I hated this. In what other art form do you show off your completely unfinished, largely unorganized work? But in the band world, that's what we do. In a typical early-season performance, students are out of step, not in uniform, missing notes, dropping flags, bumping into one another, and they may or may not be playing. It might be funny if it weren't so stressful. Not to mention, it's still 100 degrees after dusk. Friday night football lights in August. Great times.

For us, HUSTLE was a reminder that we had a lot to do and not much time to do it. It wasn't the same idea as "hustle culture," where you run yourself ragged to make as much money as possible. No. Hustle was working as hard as possible in the time that we had together. It was a rallying cry for excellence, urgency, and tenacity.

It is also a rallying cry for being a tough and tender leader. In the front of my classroom, a sign painted by a student of mine, Carolyn, read, **"Good Things Come to Those Who HUSTLE."** I think she perfectly encapsulates what is required of a tough and tender leader.

The ethic of HUSTLE is about two main ideas that I think we can all use in building culture:

1. Maximize every **minute**: We must pursue excellence.
2. Maximize every **moment:** We must pursue connection.

In the sports and arts world, we maximize **minutes** in practice and rehearsal, preparing for performances, competitions, and games. We also maximize **moments** off the field or outside of rehearsal during water breaks, locker room time, and downtime to create relationships.

In my classroom, we maximized our minutes by having a strong lesson plan, executing it to the best of our abilities, and having long-term goals for the group's excellence. However, we also maximized moments by being flexible with the plan in case the students needed more support. We even threw the plan out more than a few times if the students needed to talk about the goings-on of the school or the world, or perhaps just a moment to destress. Some of our best moments were when we would take time to do iLead lessons together, growing our leadership as a class.

In school leadership, we can maximize minutes spent developing people, creating environments where great instruction can happen, and even curating relevant professional learning experiences. We can maximize moments of connection in one-on-one meetings, lunchtime, break time, and any personal time with the people we lead.

MINUTES AND MOMENTS

Minutes and moments are BOTH important. Minutes are the toughness. Moments are the tenderness. I want to share with you some things I have learned over the years in leading an organization of minutes and moments:

1. Find time to grow every day (Minutes)

Looking at the people you are leading and telling them how you are personally growing is powerful. I like listening to podcasts and reading. My commute to work is over an hour, which allows me ample time to listen to podcasts. My car is a rolling learning studio.

Podcasts are a great way to learn about the world or gather stories to help you effectively teach yourself how to live. If you're wondering, my favorites are "Stuff You Should Know," "Revisionist History," "School on a Mission," and the "Maxwell Leadership Podcast." In my line of work, stories and leadership growth are EVERYTHING.

I also keep a book on my desk at home. I read whenever I am working from my office and need a break. Ten pages is a good break for me to clear my head and return to work.

Finally, I approach every meeting, professional development, or interaction as if someone sent that person to teach me something new. In education (you know this), we are constantly called into meetings and training that may or may not help us in our classrooms. As a music teacher, it was a near certainty that whatever it was wouldn't apply to my classroom. However, I always tried to learn.

Perhaps the person was a great communicator. I noted how they engaged their audience. It could be a new feature or platform I could adapt to use in my classroom. If both the feature and the communication were awful, I could learn how not to do things in the process. (Some people were sent here to be a negative example for others.)

Either way, I tried to learn and gain influence with my principal by being a good student.

How do you grow each day?

2. Celebrate Wins (Moments)

Do you have a folder where you keep positive notes and accolades you've received? If you don't, let me encourage you to start one. Having a record of your "wins" and regularly reviewing them is essential. Affirmation is leadership fuel. My folder of student and parent notes is HUGE and comes in handy if I'm having a bad day. It's also a great starting point if I ever need a new story to tell when I'm teaching.

Now that I'm not teaching in a classroom daily, I try to keep track of wins differently. I have saved the chat transcript from multiple Zoom training sessions where the participants were particularly pleased. Reading back over "*This is one of the best PL sessions we've ever had*" was helpful when I was stuck trying to figure out where to go next in writing this book.

Not only that, but it's also a constructive practice to see how much progress we have made.

In late 2023, I did the 75-Hard challenge. It's seventy-five days of working out twice a day, drinking a gallon of water, reading ten pages a day, following a diet, and avoiding cheat meals and alcohol. It is aptly named. (They say the most challenging part is not telling people about it; here I am, writing it into a book.)

Part of the challenge is taking a picture of yourself shirtless every day. As I took the photos, I was never quite happy with what I saw. Sometimes, it's hard to look at yourself and like what you see. However, I was blown away when I put my day one picture and day seventy-five picture next to each other. Seeing progress like that was a MAJOR win for my confidence (To see the pictures, turn to Appendix 3 – HA! Just kidding).

How do you record your wins?

3. Mind Your Body Language (Minutes)

At the end of every band rehearsal of my career, the students would chant together in what we called "Drill and Dismiss." The drum majors would shout *DRILL TO THE POSITION OF ATTENTION*, then go over the position in call and response format. It went like this:

(Drum Majors—STUDENTS):

"Heels–TOGETHER

Toes–APART

Stomach–IN

Chest–OUT

Shoulders–BACK

Chin–UP

Eyes–WITH PRIDE

Band Dismissed, Fall Out–HUSTLE!"

We did this every day because their body language was everything. How performers project from the stage, be it in a theater or on a football field, is a major determining factor in the success of a performance. Projecting confidence is vital.

You've met people like this. They walk into a room, head held high. They make eye contact with you, speak confidently, and shake your hand with a firm grip. We admire those people. They are dangerous, in a good way (Of course, sometimes they start talking and give themselves away as big dummies, but let's go with it for now.).

Band taught me this. Since my late teens, I have carried myself just as I was taught. Stomach, in. Chest, out. Shoulders, back. Chin, up. Eyes with pride. I have always tried to look confident, and that's important because looking confident helps you feel confident.

How do you project confidence?

4. Take Time to Think Before Speaking (Moments)

Charlie Houpert writes about the **30 percent rule.**[14] He says we typically only allow ourselves 30 percent of the time a listener would give us to fill a pause without it feeling awkward. We often speak too quickly, say the wrong thing, or trip over our words to move the conversation.

Great leaders give themselves time to think. This will help eliminate "interrupter" words like " um, like, or so." By choosing the right words, we project confidence in our ability to communicate well and infuse more connection and meaning into our conversations. For a leader, communication is everything, but that doesn't mean you have to speak first or fastest.

I once challenged my student leaders in this area. For two days, they had to put a quarter in a jar when they used an "interrupter" word. The pizza party we threw with the money was massive! In the process, they became more self-aware and more confident communicators.

Pause. Give yourself time to think. Make eye contact. Maximize the moment.

5. Embrace Your Flaws (Moments)

When you think about your favorite movie, TV show, or literary character, what makes them great? They have many positive attributes. They might even have superpowers! However, to make those characters more interesting, they are always given at least one weakness (Think Superman and Kryptonite). The weakness makes them more likable.

Pretending like you don't have flaws is as silly as pretending you don't have a shadow. You have both, and everyone sees both. Instead of ignoring your flaws, embrace them. People love a leader who does this. It's a key to confidence! Also, if you are ashamed of your flaws and try to hide them, you are telling yourself you are not good enough. You are admitting that parts of you are shameful to share, and you feel shame.

Admitting your flaws and owning them makes you human and more relatable.

Consider this case study:

Both Richard Nixon and John F. Kennedy Jr. made horrible errors as presidents. Nixon initiated the Watergate scandal, and Kennedy the Bay of Pigs incident. The way they handled each illustrates my point.

Nixon never admitted he did wrong. He famously said, "I am not a crook" when asked about his involvement, and in an interview with David Frost in 1977, went so far as to say, "When the President does it, that means it's not illegal."[15] As Nixon left office, he sported the lowest approval rating in Presidential History (24 percent). [16]

Kennedy, however, handled his situation differently. Kennedy took full responsibility after the botched operation in Cuba, saying, "*There's an old saying that victory has 100 fathers and defeat is an orphan. Further statements, detailed discussions, are not to conceal responsibility because I'm the responsible officer of the government...*"[17] As a result of this ownership, his approval rating reached an astronomical 83 Percent![18] Admitting he had made an error endeared him to those he was leading.

Embrace your flaws.

EPIC HUSTLE

My friend Carlos was the basketball coach at Delta College in Michigan for a long time. He is a great man, a great coach, and a great leader. He used to tell his players to be EPIC, meaning "Every Play is Crucial." EPIC for Delta College meant making the most of every opportunity. He even asked his players how they were going to be EPIC off the court. Sometimes, that was serving the community. Other times, it was simply holding the doors for classmates to walk through. Nothing was too small to be EPIC. Carlos was a master of getting his players to maximize their minutes and moments.

That's what HUSTLE was for my team. To become tough and tender and lead people into saying, "I LOVE THIS PLACE," we must maximize every minute and moment we get. It's not about extra work. It's about the quality of the work. It's not about doing more. It's about doing better.

Over the years, HUSTLE expanded to represent our core values as an organization. We gave each letter of the word a name, and in the process, we developed a unique culture where we trained, retained, and recruited more students as leaders.

Humility
Understanding
Scholarship
Trust
Leadership
Excellence

The journey to becoming a tough and tender leader starts with HUSTLE.

There's a strategy for the order of the words in HUSTLE. Of course, it's helpful that it spells a word. Truth be told, the word came first. But we are often led to great things by accident. I believe that these words appear in the best order possible.

Humility and **Understanding** come first. We must build a team based on inclusion and belonging. This is essential in culture building because a leader with no followers is just a person going for a walk. Leadership requires being approachable to those you lead.

Being humble creates a sense of community around you. You recognize your strengths and your faults, and you bring people on board who complement you. Being humble also lets people know that you're not a leader who's all about yourself.

Being a leader who is understanding means that you look at your team and their diverse backgrounds, strengths, and unique experiences, and you leverage them for the good of all. As you will see later, a team full of differences is really good to have around you when making decisions. Discovering people's strengths and giving them the opportunity to use them is essential for building teams of leaders.

Next, we show them that we can do a great job. That's **scholarship**. When I say scholarship, I mean you study your craft and execute it well. That includes teaching, administration, coaching, leadership, and any other role you are required to fulfill. There is no substitute for doing a good job.

After people see that you are a scholar of your craft and you've shown that you care through humility and understanding, you're beginning to establish **trust**. **Trust** allows you to deliver feedback with candor to those you lead (and vice versa; they will give you the feedback you need to grow).

As we do the above four things, we build better **leadership** habits and attitudes. Your leadership habits will help you determine the direction of your life and career. Your leadership attitude will determine who's standing next to you as you progress through the milestones of that journey. When we demonstrate that we are here for one another and that our mission is to lead each other well good things happen.

Finally, **excellence** is a by-product of the first five. It would be difficult to imagine a place where the leaders are humble, understanding, scholarly, trusting, leading well, and that place didn't display excellence. By excellence, I don't mean test scores and evaluation ratings. Those are important, but they are not enduring.

An atmosphere of excellence that celebrates progress, growth, and leadership will endure long after the test scores, trophies, and certificates of achievement have faded. When I talk about leadership excellence, I am talking about a commitment level to each other that goes beyond quantitative data. We will learn together that excellence is everywhere and in everyone; it simply requires a culture that finds and celebrates it.

TOUGH AND TENDER HUSTLE

There happen to be three of each value dedicated to Toughness and Tenderness:

Tender	Tough
Humility	Scholarship
Understanding	Leadership
Trust	Excellence

When I look at the tenets of leadership that make up HUSTLE, a well-rounded approach to great leadership appears. Not only are these areas in which I need to grow, but they are also characteristics I crave in those who lead me. These are values I hope to grow in my students and in my children.

One of the culture-building rituals that we built into our organization was the creation of the HUSTLE award for students. When we adopted these values for our organization, we needed some way to honor students and staff who showed dedication to living them out. This was not an award with an arbitrary rubric. It was not a popularity contest like most awards seem to be. It was an award that anyone could win if they took the values of HUSTLE and applied them to their life.

To win the HUSTLE award, a student or staff member had to display **humility** by dedicating themselves to serving their community in some way. This could be through some of our in-school initiatives or something outside, through their church, scouts, or another organization. (Humility was the HU in HUSTLE when we started; we added understanding later.)

The students had to show **scholarship** by maintaining a certain GPA. I wanted them to understand the importance of doing their best in their classes as a way to influence others.

They had to show **trust** by getting fellow students and teachers to fill out recommendations for them. Each applicant had to get four peers and one teacher to vouch for their trustworthiness. This was a good lesson for many of them that their leadership mattered beyond the band room and even beyond school.

The students grew their **leadership** habits and attitudes by attending after-school leadership workshops that we hosted once a week for an entire semester. We wanted to see a dedication to learning how to lead and an attitude of solving problems and serving people.

Finally, students showed **excellence** by taking private lessons on their instrument, auditioning for the all-region/all-state band, and performing a solo on their instrument at the district festival each year.

I was interested in their individual development as musicians and how that influenced their peers. Creating a culture of excellence through individual skills was how we chose to grow the program. This paid enormous dividends for us in that every student saw that they could be an excellent musician, and once that became expected of them, it became part of our culture.

It wasn't about winning the solo contest or being first in the region or state. We made sure they knew that this step was about them taking ownership of their growth, encouraging others to join them, and for them to have the courage to put themselves out there as a leader.

Each year at our banquet, we would give out the HUSTLE awards at the very end. I got the biggest medallions I could find, so the students felt special. I encouraged them to wear them at graduation (because our medals were the biggest), and since they could win the HUSTLE award each year, some of them walked at graduation with four medallions.

Celebrating these incredible leaders was a highlight of the year. It allowed others to see that anyone could be a leader.

Anyone can participate in building a culture of leadership. From the time we started giving the award each year, I saw an increasing number of students vying to complete the requirements. And each year, our culture got a little better, our recruiting classes got a little bigger, and our retention percentage grew (I'll present data on how effective these initiatives were at the end of the book.).

Long story short, the framework of HUSTLE will help you become a tough and tender leader, and will also give you lessons, metaphors, and resources to share with your team. I hope you come away from these next chapters energized about your leadership and excited about developing leaders around you.

Each of the following chapters will explore the six tenets of HUSTLE in more detail. You may approach them in any order; however, I firmly believe they work best in the order I have presented them. I leave it to you to decide.

Happy HUSTLING.

THE 1-4-3 – CHAPTER 4: "GOOD THINGS COME TO THOSE WHO HUSTLE"

1 Quotable Quote

"Maximize every minute by pursuing excellence. Maximize every moment by pursuing connection."

Leadership isn't about doing more—it's about doing the right things with the time and people you've got. HUSTLE is your compass.

4 Key Takeaways

1. **Minutes vs. Moments:** Strong leaders value time (minutes) and value people (moments). Both are needed.
2. **HUSTLE = Six Core Values of Tough and Tender Leadership:** The acronym stands for Humility, Understanding, Scholarship, Trust, Leadership, and Excellence.
3. **Work Smart, Not Just Hard:** Hustle isn't about burnout—it's about focus, clarity, and shared values that drive sustainable excellence.
4. **Leadership is Visible:** Body language, communication habits, and personal growth all influence how others perceive and follow you.

3 Questions for Your Team

1. How are you maximizing your minutes (planning, strategy, systems) and your moments (connection, presence, encouragement)?
2. Which part of HUSTLE comes most naturally to you—and which one needs your attention right now?
3. How would your students or teammates describe the way you show up daily—in your effort, energy, and presence?

5

Humility – "Turn Your Back to the Crowd"

GREAT LEADERSHIP OFTEN starts by admitting that leadership is not about me. I must accurately view myself and what I bring to the table. I have many strengths but also many weaknesses. By leaning into my strengths, I know what I'm capable of and can confidently act. By being honest about my weaknesses, I can be humble enough to ask others for help.

Remember, leadership requires other people. It can never be about just me. Imagine a softball coach sitting in the dugout without players because they didn't show up. Or imagine a conductor leading an orchestra of empty chairs. That's what my job would have looked like if I hadn't influenced my students to let me lead them.

Being a Band Director for so many years taught me a lot about humility. I'm unsure if you have ever been a part of a musical ensemble, much less conducted one. Conducting music is one of my favorite things to do. It's a dance. If you move and direct well, and the musicians follow, it's an experience.

Conducting is non-verbal communication. I can't shout directions over the music for them to hear (this one time, a group of freshmen got it from me mid-concert, but I digress). No, I must lead them with my hands, baton, body position, and face to influence them to make beautiful music together.

All of this occurs with my back to the audience.

It's a beautiful picture of humble leadership. For music making to happen, I do most of the work: planning rehearsals, studying materials, assigning parts, and managing people (answering parent emails, oy vey, the parent emails). But during the performance, I must be willing to turn my back to the crowd and let the musicians shine. I must confidently lead them and humbly get out of their way.

The metaphor doesn't only apply to music. If you've seen any of your coaching colleagues who work with their players, they are likely very hands-on in practice, but at the games, the players must do the work. The coach remains on the sideline, providing guidance, but it's the players that the fans cheer for (we rarely cheer for the coach… yet don't we often blame them for the failings of the team?).

To reframe this idea, our practices can't happen without us there. But if we've done our job well, the performances can. In fact, the most remarkable performances we ever gave were ones where I did very little on the podium and allowed the students to make music together. Talk about connection!

GROWING IN HUMILITY

Growing in humility is often a challenge for leaders. Many people want us to believe that humility is weak. They say leaders should take charge, be outgoing, and tell others what to do. True leadership strength comes from being as humble as possible.

Adam Grant, an organizational psychologist and professor at the University of Pennsylvania's Wharton School, agrees, saying:

"Every[one] should learn that humility and kindness aren't signs of weakness. They're strengths of character. Recognizing your faults doesn't mean you lack self-esteem. It shows you have self-awareness. Showing compassion doesn't mean you lack backbone. It shows you have heart."[19]

Any leader afraid to admit their faults is in for a rough ride. Think of those who lead you. Are you aware of their faults? I'm sure you are. You probably have a file ready if they ever asked to see them.

I once asked my students to list my faults as an experiment. Ten minutes later, I had to ask them to stop! The people we lead know we are imperfect. The strength to admit imperfection gains you influence, not vice versa.

In his book *8 Paradoxes of Great Leadership*, my friend Dr. Tim Elmore gives us a picture of how to become a humbler leader.

He says, humble leaders "listen more than they speak, learn more than they are taught, and seek to add more value than they gain."[20]

Try these three steps to become a humbler leader:

1. The people you lead want to be heard.
   Listen to them.
2. They want to share their successes and struggles.
   Learn from them.
3. They want to be supported and know they have value.
   Add value to them.

Like a music teacher or a coach who does much of the work preparing and empowering the people they lead, we must do the same. We must also be willing to share the credit or even give it to others when the opportunity arises. I would often tell our students and parents "*when things are going well, it's because we have great students and staff doing wonderful things. If things are going poorly, I will apologize for not preparing them well enough.*"

This picture of humility earned me a lot of influence on students and parents. How can you take a similar approach to those you lead?

TRUST YOUR SKILLS

Turning your back to the crowd does not mean denying your ability to lead. We must also trust our leadership skills. Simply being willing to work together with others, admit your faults, and take the blame when things go wrong will not get people to say, "I LOVE THIS PLACE." People want to know their leaders are competent and confident.

Confidence supercharges humility. It is contagious. A confident leader energizes their team, motivates them, and gives them ownership. Confidence doesn't have to be loud. All too often, we mistake charisma for leadership. That was certainly the case in my early career. Extroverts get a lot of the credit for leadership, but introverts are just as likely to get the job done.

My colleague at Growing Leaders, Melissa, is a perfect example of this. She is a quiet force in our office. You'd never know it, but every person on our team goes to her for advice, counsel, and discernment. She's not the outgoing, microphone-loving leader that I am. But truly, our team could not function without her leadership.

In fact, some of the most outstanding leaders in our history have been introverts:

1. Albert Einstein
2. Rosa Parks
3. Bill Gates
4. Steven Spielberg
5. Isaac Newton
6. Eleanor Roosevelt
7. Barack Obama
8. Meryl Streep

The famous actor Marlon Brando once said, "Confidence is silent. Insecurities are Loud." This type of confidence is well-suited to humility.

HUMILITY PREVENTS YOUR CONFIDENCE FROM BECOMING ARROGANCE

The pairing of humility and confidence is essential. Humility without confidence leads to the leader being a doormat (or cotton candy). We can't be effective if we are being overrun. Confidence unchecked by humility leads to arrogance (Hello, Mr. Drill Sergeant). Leading with arrogance is a great way to get people to look for other jobs.

Being tough and tender means embracing both confidence and humility. In fact, humility does four things to temper confidence to keep you from becoming arrogant.

1. **Humility invites others to join you.** This alone will prevent others from seeing you as arrogant.
2. **Humility strengthens your confidence.** It becomes more believable when you invite others in.
3. **Humility relieves the leader of the burden of knowing it all.** There's a lot of pressure to know everything. Humility sheds that burden.
4. **Humility allows for shared credit and lessens the pain of blame.** Shared credit makes for a great team. It helps others forgive you for your mistakes.

Often, when I see arrogant leaders, I ask myself, "What are they hiding from?" In many cases, those leaders are trying to control the situation around them and hide from their flaws. If they are in full control, they can't be let down by others. But we cannot hide from humility. If we don't embrace it, its cousin, humiliation, may show up.

HUMILITY'S TOUGH COUSIN, HUMILIATION

Humility and humiliation come from the same root noun in Greek, "Humilitas." "Humilis" is its adjective form. The word means grounded or "from the earth." We sometimes say a humble person is **grounded** (Or perhaps we ground our children to humble them.).

Metaphorically, "from the earth" means that we all come from and go to the same place. It's a reminder that no one is better or worse than another. Being grounded means you understand your value in relation to others.

You likely understand the meaning of the word humiliation from personal experience. Once, early in my career, I was serving as an adjunct teacher for a local High School band. Their leader, Gary Gribble, was a seasoned veteran teacher whom I love and respect still to this day. At one practice, late in the season, I disagreed with one of the older students. He was eighteen, and I may have been twenty-two at the time. Not too far apart. I had given him instructions that he didn't like. He raised his hand and asked Mr. Gribble about it, and Mr. Gribble (who didn't know about our disagreement) sided with the student.

I was furious. How dare this young man defy me? I went straight to Mr. Gribble afterward and told him what had happened, gave all my magnanimous reasons why I was right, and told him to fix it for me. He gently refused, but I pushed back even harder. At that moment, Gary looked at me and asked how far I planned to go with this, and wondered how, in my few years of teaching, I had gotten so confident in my abilities. He (kindly) asked why I was so hell-bent on getting my way with a five-second portion of an eight-minute production.

His perspective on the situation helped me see that I was acting childishly. It wasn't a big deal, and in hindsight, the student was right. I didn't like having my ideas challenged. I was humiliated by my behavior and apologized to Gary and the student for being so abrasive to them both. It was not my finest moment.

Humiliation is finding the ground through means other than self-reflection. Someone shows you your faults, calls you out, or puts you in your place. At its worst, you find out how people feel about you after a long time has passed (Or you visit ratemyteacher.com).

Leaders find themselves grounded in one of two ways. They either humbly accept their flaws, invite others to fill their gaps, build teams, and empower others or they find themselves grounded by others, through humiliation. This could be in a meeting, being called out by a peer or a boss. It could be by a parent's email or phone call, letting you know your leadership isn't up to par. Perhaps a social media post or group is dedicated to the ineffectiveness of a leader. It could even be at a retirement ceremony or party, where few even bother to show up.

We will all find the ground one way or another. Pretending that we do not have flaws, are irreplaceable, or are generally arrogant will inevitably lead to humiliation. Great leaders, tough and tender leaders, lean into humility.

Humble leaders draw others in by being self-aware. As they do, those people will start to love the place and the leader. Recently, I came across an amazing example of humility and self-awareness on the biggest possible stage. Let's talk football.

THE GREATEST PLAY OF SUPER BOWL 57 (THAT NO ONE TALKS ABOUT)

Super Bowl 57 was one of the more tightly contested games in National Football League championship history. The game featured several fascinating narratives worth mentioning.

First, it pitted the top two seeds from each league and the two teams with the best regular-season records. This meant, to the fans, it should be a well-played game. The game also featured brothers Jason and Travis Kelce facing off as opponents on opposite sides of the ball.

Chiefs Coach Andy Reid was leading his team against the team that gave him his start. He was the head coach of the Eagles from 1999-2012 before being let go, only to find himself at the helm of the Chiefs in Kansas City.

Finally, it was the first game in Super Bowl history to feature two black starting Quarterbacks, Jalen Hurts and Patrick Mahomes. Both were Pro Bowl players during the season and were finalists for the league's Most Valuable Player award, which Mahomes eventually won.

As the game neared the end of the fourth quarter, fans were treated to a tie game, each team netting thirty-five points. The chance to see the game decided in overtime was on everyone's mind. Everyone except for Reid, Mahomes, and a journeyman running back named Jerrick McKinnon.

McKinnon's Super Bowl stats weren't notable. He managed only three receptions for fifteen yards and no touchdowns. And he only carried the ball four times for thirty-four yards. The stats make it easy to assume McKinnon had little effect on the game's outcome. That assumption would be incorrect. McKinnon had the most crucial play of the entire Super Bowl.

Just after the two-minute warning in the fourth quarter, it looked as if the Chiefs would score to take a 42-35 lead over the Eagles. But the Chiefs faced a real problem. Their offense was firing on all cylinders, but so was the Eagles'. And if you looked at the KC sidelines, you would have seen an exhausted group of men on defense. If the Chiefs score quickly, the Eagles will have plenty of time to return the favor. And if they head to overtime, it is anyone's game.

With 1:48 left on the clock, Mahomes handed the ball off to Jerrick McKinnon. To everyone watching, McKinnon was headed for the end zone to score and celebrate with his team. McKinnon, however, had other plans.

Remarkably, as he approached the end zone, he slid, stopping the play at the one-yard line. Brilliant strategy! By not scoring, he allowed his team to run out the clock and kick a field goal. The Chiefs took a 38-35 lead with eight seconds left, and the world watched as Jerrick McKinnon (with his mere forty-nine yards) and his team were crowned Super Bowl Champions.

McKinnon NOT scoring was the difference in the game.

Imagine the stories that Jerrick McKinnon could have told his kids and grandkids. "Kids, sit a spell while I tell you how grandpappy scored a touchdown in the Super Bowl." (I know you read that in the same voice I did.) He could have played the video of the scoring play and ensuing celebration at family reunions and parties. He would have been celebrated as a hero in Kansas City and back in his hometown of Marietta, Georgia (where I taught).

But the outcome of the game could have just as likely been the opposite: McKinnon scores, the Eagles get the ball back and go on to win. In this scenario, not only would McKinnon's TD have gone unnoticed, but he also wouldn't be a champion.

Jerrick McKinnon did exactly what a leader does when they turn their back to the crowd. He chose his team over personal glory. He displayed great humility in his willingness NOT to score.

After the game, McKinnon said, "It wasn't even a hesitation in my mind once I knew the situation we were in. We practice that every week. I've been waiting my entire life to be a Super Bowl Champion,"[21] he said.

We can learn a lot about humble and confident leadership from Jerrick McKinnon.

THE 1-4-3 – CHAPTER 5: HUMILITY – "TURN YOUR BACK TO THE CROWD"

1 Quotable Quote

"Humble leaders draw others in by being self-aware. As they do, those people will start to love the place and the leader."

Humility isn't about being small—it's about leading in a way that lifts others higher than you. That's where real influence begins.

4 Key Takeaways

1. **Humility Builds Influence:** Leaders gain trust by owning mistakes, giving credit, and listening more than they speak.
2. **Turn Your Back to the Crowd:** Like a conductor, leaders lead best when they empower others and stay focused on the mission, not the spotlight.
3. **Humility Needs Confidence:** The two must work together—unchecked confidence becomes arrogance, while humility without confidence leads to passivity.
4. **Humiliation Is the Alternative:** Leaders who don't choose humility may eventually be humbled by circumstances or others.

3 Questions for Your Team

1. What does "turn your back to the crowd" mean in your role?
2. Where are you modeling humility in ways your students or staff can actually see?
3. How do you balance confidence with not becoming arrogant?

6

Understanding – "Leading Your Symphony"

FOR SIXTEEN YEARS, I was lucky enough to teach across the hall from an incredible educator and friend, Dr. David Doke. Dave was also the director of our orchestra. Our orchestra was fantastic, and Dave loved taking the musicians on trips to showcase their talents to broad audiences. They gave concerts at the Kennedy Center in Washington, DC, Symphony Hall in Chicago, and Carnegie Hall in New York City.

One of the last and greatest opportunities that I had was when Dr. Doke invited me to conduct the orchestra in Carnegie Hall. In the Spring of 2021, we took a full symphony (strings, winds, and percussion) to New York City to perform. Dave asked me if I would conduct the Finale to Antonín Dvořák's *Symphony No. 9*, "From the New World." You've probably heard it; the opening sounds a lot like the "Jaws" theme.

Putting that concert together was an incredibly challenging and meaningful experience. When you think about it, the symphony orchestra is a diverse team of people and sounds. You have the familiar strains of the string family with its violins and cellos, to the pastoral wanderings of the woodwinds, like the flutes and oboes. Not to mention the power of the brass section, with its trumpets and trombones, and the percussion section, its timpani and cymbals calling forth sounds reminiscent of battle. Dvořák used them all in the New World Symphony, and our students gave an amazing and memorable performance.

The power of the symphony is in the diversity of its voices. Let's contrast that with a soloist.

There is something wonderful and intimate about a solo performance. It could be an acoustic guitar with a vocalist in the park on a cool fall night or a single trumpeter playing the fanfare of a bride's entrance. As a trumpet player myself, I have played numerous weddings. There's an awesome power and responsibility of playing by yourself in moments of great emotional weight, like a bridal entrance.

The soloist is courageous and wonderful. They can wow you with their virtuosity and draw you in with their softness. However, they are limited to what one person can do. A soloist cannot do what a symphony can.

While soloists and symphonies can both make beautiful music, only the symphony can encompass the range of emotions, sounds, power, and volume that encapsulates the human experience.

The symphony is powerful because of its range. Its diversity of voices, each one playing to its strengths, taking center stage when needed and fading to the background to allow others to have the spotlight (This is tough for trumpet players, like me, who always want the spotlight).

Gustav Mahler once said, "A symphony must be like the world. It must contain everything."[22] His vision for the orchestra's operation is a perfect metaphor for our next step in becoming a tough and tender leader.

As school leaders, we must develop an understanding of the diversity and strengths of the people in our building. A school building is full of teams—sports teams, administrative teams, collaborative teams, clubs, cliques, and shared interests. One of my favorite parts about working in a school was getting to know the diverse makeup and culture of each team we had. And with the right leadership, we can turn that diversity into a major strength.

THREE WAYS TO CULTIVATE UNDERSTANDING ON YOUR TEAM

Our band had four different classes differentiated by ability that met every day. In addition, we had the marching band, the drumline, the color guard, the jazz band, the pit orchestra, and the percussion ensemble. Each group was composed of and led by different people with different interests, strengths, and backgrounds. Maximizing each group's potential required the leaders to get to know the members and understand their needs and goals.

It was extra work, but it was worth it.

When you work in elective classes, students can elect to return or exit each year. Our jobs depended on creating an environment where students wanted to join and stay for all four years.

The more numbers we recruited, the more job security we had. This is why culture was so important. Remember, based on culture and leadership, people choose to stay, leave, engage, or tune out. It's true in the arts, and it's true across the spectrum of educational leadership.

Over the years, I have learned that understanding the people I was leading meant three things.

Great leaders:

1. Embrace diversity as an advantage.
2. Cultivate belonging.
3. Leverage the strengths of those they lead.

EMBRACING DIVERSITY AS AN ADVANTAGE

When you think of diversity, you likely think of what you can see. That makes sense; these types of diversity are the ones we discuss most. Gender and skin color come to mind. However, there's much more to diversity than that.

Staffing agency *Insight Global* recognizes twenty-three different types of diversity in the workplace:

1. Race
2. Ethnicity
3. Gender
4. Physical/Mental Ability
5. Age
6. Sexual Orientation
7. Geography
8. Income
9. Personal Habits
10. Recreational Interests
11. Religion/Spirituality
12. Education
13. Work Experience
14. Appearance
15. Parental Status
16. Marital Status
17. Job Title
18. Content Field
19. Division/Dept
20. Seniority
21. Work Location
22. Union Affiliation
23. Management Status

Granted, some of these are more difficult to talk about than others, but it is worth noting that we can experience diversity in several ways. For example:

I am a white, middle-aged, Southern, middle-class man. I am educated and have nearly two decades of teaching experience. I am of average height. I'm balding (I like to say I have "wavy" hair… it's waving goodbye). I love to exercise and to read. I love the Georgia Bulldogs, the Atlanta Falcons, and the Atlanta Braves (even after decades of heartbreak). I am a father of two boys and have been married for over twenty years since finishing this book. You know, by now, I was a music teacher, which was very different from teaching a core academic subject because we didn't have standardized tests and end-of-course exams like my peers. I got to set my own curricular standards, scope, and sequence.

I tell you all these things to point out that I have a particular lens of experiences from which to draw my worldview. If I only rely on my point of view and perspective, I become like the soloist from the opening of this chapter. I can do certain things very well, but I will always be limited (a funnel, if you will). I must be willing to look to others' strengths and perspectives to enrich my life and the culture around me.

Of course, we experience diversity in many ways. A person on your team is much more than their skin color or gender (this is not to downplay any one item, but to expand the appreciation of the many ways in which we are diverse).

We leaders must understand that our team's composition is just as essential as its competence. We all want to work on high-performing teams that get things done and move the needle toward progress. Sometimes, we forget that the people we work with are just as important as the goals we are working toward.

The intelligence platform Cloverpop joined forces with Bain and Company to do several studies on diversity. One study found that "Diversity can increase friction [between teammates] by 15 percent.[23]" That doesn't sound good.

However, they also found that "inclusion boosts results by 60 percent." I'm no math guy, but that sounds like it's good. The friction is worthwhile because it boosts results (tough leaders are thrilled; they love results). Including people in decision-making processes can make the process more challenging and time-consuming, but it leads to better outcomes.

Erik Larson writes, "Inclusion instantly activates existing age, gender, and geographic diversity for better decision-making." He also found that while teams of people make better decisions than individuals 66 percent of the time, <u>diverse</u> teams improve that to 87 percent.[24]

In that same study by Cloverpop, they found that the worst decisions were made by all-male leadership teams and executed by a diverse workforce. The best decisions were made by teams that included age, gender, and geographic diversity.[25]

Business management consulting firm Deloitte found that "diversity increases innovation by 20%, improves decision-making quality by 20%, and reduces risk by 30%."[26]

The symphony is more powerful than the soloist in making decisions and innovating. When you consider the amount of diversity in the school environment as compared to the business environment (just the addition of students expands the potential), shouldn't we embrace diversity as an advantage?

Whenever I think about how diversity helps with decision-making, I think about my time as the Fine Arts Department chair at our school. Our department chair meetings were full of diverse voices. We had teachers from each content area (music, theater, visual art), multiple levels of experience, and a lot (and I truly mean a lot) of opinions. Our meetings often felt longer than they should be, and decisions sometimes came at a slow pace. But in the end, I look back on those meetings and truly feel that the friction created by our decision-making process and the diverse voices led to better decisions. We were often able to bring better ideas forward and even protect our department from potentially bad ideas. Diverse teams can be slow, but the process is worth it. As John Maxwell says, "If you want to go fast, go alone. If you want to go far, go with others."

However, bringing diverse voices and perspectives together isn't quite enough to develop the leadership quality of understanding. We, as leaders, must also cultivate a sense of belonging in our teams and schools. We can't just bring people together; we need them to know their voices matter and that they belong, and sometimes we need help finding common ground.

CULTIVATE BELONGING

In May of 2023, Surgeon General Vivek Murthy released an eighty-five-page advisory declaring loneliness a new public health epidemic in the US. That report stated, "Our epidemic of loneliness and isolation has been an underappreciated public health crisis that has harmed individual and societal health. Our relationships are a source of healing and well-being, hiding in plain sight—one that can help us live healthier, more fulfilled, and more productive lives…"[27]

The findings of the study show that the effects of loneliness are as harmful as smoking and have a lasting impact on mental health, leading to an increased risk of heart disease, stroke, and dementia.

The risk is most significant in our schools.

In a report by CNBC in 2020, it was found that 73 percent of Generation Z say they feel alone sometimes or always.[28] This is the highest of any generation. Second to Gen Z in loneliness came Millennials. Remember, those are your students and many (perhaps most) of your teachers.

There is also a stigma surrounding loneliness that makes it difficult to discuss.

We are more connected today than at any time in our history. Social media and online gaming allow anyone to connect at any time. My own children will tell me they're going to hang out with their friends. Do they leave the house? No. They head to their gaming consoles in the basement. The mistake we often make is thinking those online connections are a good substitute for genuine human connection.

Your students and much of your staff are younger than Google. They have likely never been offline in their lives. Creating a connection between them is an essential task for any leader.

Cultivating belonging sounds challenging, but I can offer a simple solution. First, let me tell you about the front row of my classroom in 2021.

Musical ensembles are generally set up in rows. Quieter instruments are in the front; louder instruments are in the back. Drums? As far away as possible… lol. This setup is mainly pragmatic, allowing for an outstanding sound balance.

LESSONS FROM THE FRONT ROW

In the front row of my mastery-level class in my final year of teaching, there were nine students: two clarinet players, four flute players, two oboe players, and one bassoonist. That alone was diversity, but let’s look at the people. The students in that front row were tall, short, Black, White, Asian, male, and female. They were blonde, brunette, and red-headed. They were athletes, thespians, and ROTC students. They came from nuclear families, single-parent homes, and one was adopted. Some had high levels of confidence, while others really struggled with self-esteem.

I say all of this to point out the sheer diversity in the front row alone! And I was as different from them as they were from each other. I could go on about every student in that class. There was a trumpet player who was the captain of the cross-country team. Another young man was on the defensive line on the football team and played in the trombone section. One young lady was a lovely, autistic clarinet player who spoke her mind at every turn.

Our groups were full of diversity.

As with any symphony-like group, it was my job to get them to work together. I also had to make them feel like they belonged so they could achieve great results and share in that success. But how? While embracing diversity is about recognizing and embracing what makes us different, **cultivating belonging is about remembering what makes us all the same.**

John Maxwell's 101 percent principle is a secret weapon for cultivating belonging in our schools. It transcends all borders and boundaries and will help leaders create an environment where everyone can feel like they have a place.

The 101 percent principle says, "We must find the 1 percent we have in common and give it 100 percent of our efforts."[29] In a world that tends to focus on differences, this principle reminds us that belonging focuses on what makes us the same.

In 2019, Paul Hanel and a team of researchers found that our beliefs and values are similar globally. People of differing religions are 91 percent similar. There is a 96 percent similarity between the rich and the poor. There is a 96 percent similarity between genders. Ninety-six percent between age groups, and 97 percent between education levels.[30] We are more alike than we are different. This is comforting.*

Cultivating belonging is about bringing people together. We pull apart from one another when we focus only on the ways we are different, creating "us versus them" situations. Belonging helps us get past that thinking.

Our "1 percent" was that we were in the band together at Hillgrove High School. That was our common bond. We could use that as a foundation, so everyone had a place. The trumpets weren't more important than the percussion (As a trumpet player, that statement is REALLY hard to write.). Everyone had a role and a purpose in the group.

I had a phrase that we used in recruiting pitches to middle school students and their parents that I think encapsulates this perfectly:

"There is someone just like you waiting for someone just like you."

Belonging requires finding what we have in common with everyone on our team. Everyone can find someone who is like them. Every teammate has something in common with every other teammate. I felt so strongly about this concept that our leadership got together and wrote it into our vision statement: "Music is our common bond. We envision a world in which young musicians grow into life-giving leaders in whatever profession they choose."

The flutes in the front row and the timpanist in the back are still a part of the same symphony.

Once you take steps to cultivate team belonging, it's time to figure out what each team member does best and give them opportunities to lead others and make progress using those strengths. As leaders, delegating to team members based on their strengths and passions is the fast lane to influencing and improving culture.

LEVERAGE THE STRENGTHS OF THOSE YOU LEAD

My friend and basketball coach, Ed Morris, once told me about a player named CJ. He and his fellow coaches were very close to cutting CJ from the team at the end of his Junior year. They felt his attitude and effort weren't what they should be for a rising senior. However, at the end of each season, the coaching staff would interview players to find out what went well and what needed to be improved. When coach Morris asked his players, "Who on the team sets the best screens?" each of them answered, "CJ does it best, Coach."

Coach Morris was dumbfounded. How is it that the player he was about to cut was unanimously seen as the best screener on the team? Instead of cutting CJ, Coach Morris challenged him. He told CJ the team needed him to be the best screener on the court. CJ responded in practice and games and ended up starting every game during his senior year! The power of finding his strength led to amazing, even unexpected results.

You may agree that focusing on strengths is not something we do very well in education. Here's a case study. A student shares with you their report card. They say, "I got As in science, social studies, art, and literature. Bs in graphic arts and Spanish. And a C in Math." What are you likely to say? "You need to get to work on that math grade."

We live in a culture of "fixing." This starts very early in our learning journey, around fourth grade, where I live, because that's when we begin to give percentages and letter grades. We see the "wrong" things and want to work on them. My classroom management skills are weak, so I need to focus on improving them. My math grade is low, so I must study math more.

We are like this in relationships as well, aren't we? If my wife comes to me with a problem, I want to fix it. That's how I see myself being helpful. Over the years, she's learned to tell me that she needs me to listen, not fix. She's got it handled; she only wants to share (If anything, I'm what needs fixing.).

What if we spent more time focusing on our strengths and less time trying to improve our weaknesses?

One of my favorite new fields of study is Positive Psychology. Founded by Martin Seligman, Positive Psychology focuses on what is going right with people and using those insights and tools to move past coping and toward thriving.

In a study related to this idea, Gallup found that employees feel more confident, self-aware, and productive when focusing on strengths rather than weaknesses. This leads to higher engagement, increased performance, and lower attrition rates.[31]

That sounds like a bunch of folks saying I LOVE THIS PLACE to me!

Building strength-focused leadership teams could be the missing ingredient to a highly successful culture! Elif Suner, a leadership and development coach writing for Forbes, says strength-based approaches typically demand only two things of the leaders in charge:

1. Leaders must intentionally focus on strengths over weaknesses.
2. Developing awareness by using tools for assessing strengths before implementing them.[32]

In short, prioritize strengths and use tools to help people to discover them.

There are many strength assessments out there. My favorite is the Six Types of Working Genius, put together by the Table Group, led by Patrick Lencioni. This study reveals that each of us has a "genius": two areas that energize us when we work in them. They call weaknesses 'working frustrations', meaning I can do them (and often must), but they will drain or frustrate me.

The six geniuses are Wonder, Invention, Discernment, Galvanizing, Enablement, and Tenacity. I am high in Invention and Tenacity. I love to make things better, and once I start something, I will finish it (Though writing this book has tested both of these geniuses.).

My Working Genius assessment describes me as a *Methodical Architect*: "A precise, reliable, and planful solver of problems. A unique combination of innovative thinking and practical implementation." I love that description.

My working frustrations are enablement and discernment. I am drained by being asked to drop what I'm doing to help or to take time to find out why something doesn't work. I can do those things, and I must. But I also must recognize that they are going to drain me (Hires an editor immediately.).

We did this exercise together as a team at Growing Leaders, and it was very eye-opening. Our team covers all six geniuses (and frustrations). We have used the Working Genius assessment to solidify our roles and better understand each other.

Strength-focused teams function better for four reasons:

1. They **listen** to each other because **understanding** is a priority.
2. They **appreciate** one another because they **know** each other.
3. They **share** the workload, allowing each team member to showcase their **strengths**.
4. They **delegate**, lowering each person's chance of **burning out**.

By becoming strengths-focused, we can increase results and belonging and decrease workload and burnout. This is due in large part to the fact that by delegating tasks, my team members' strengths can offset my weaknesses (and vice versa). This isn't an excuse not to grow in our areas of weakness; by working together to offset those weaknesses, a strength-focused team allows me to grow without it being at the expense of others.

FINDING BALANCE

When we were preparing for that performance in Carnegie Hall, we practiced in two different spaces: the orchestra room and the stage. Unfortunately, neither of those rooms had the acoustics that Carnegie Hall does. As a result, we spent most of our time on balance. Balance in music is the idea that each voice in the orchestra must adjust its volume and intensity to match its priority in the music at that time. Sometimes, we need to hear the violins loudest. Other times, it’s the oboe, the flutes, or the French Horns.

The thing about finding balance is that it’s all about creating an atmosphere for each voice to shine. When the violins are the focus, the other voices don’t have to change too much. There are a lot of violins. There will be no problem with them projecting to the audience in Carnegie Hall.

However, when there is an oboe solo in the middle of the piece, everyone in the orchestra must make a significant volume adjustment for the sound to be heard clearly. You see, the strength of the oboe is its beauty and uniqueness of sound, not its volume. We spent a lot of time helping the team understand why the oboe was important in that passage and what adjustments were necessary for the performance to be successful. It wasn't that the other voices didn't belong; we just needed to set the environment for the oboe to shine.

The culture you're creating, this feeling of I LOVE THIS PLACE, is a lot like finding balance in an orchestral performance. The success of your team and school culture hinges on the people you're leading feeling that they are seen and heard. They must know when they are essential and when they need to step back and support others. Tough and tender leaders must have an understanding of people's passions, talents, skills, and strengths.

THE 1-4-3 – CHAPTER 6: UNDERSTANDING – "LEADING YOUR SYMPHONY"

1 Quotable Quote

"The power of the symphony is in the diversity of its voices."

It's not just about getting diverse voices in the room—it's about tuning the environment so everyone can play to their strengths.

4 Key Takeaways

1. **Our Differences Are Our Strength:** Teams improve when leaders actively seek out and embrace a wide range of perspectives and backgrounds.
2. **Belonging is Crucial:** People stay and engage where they feel connected—belonging is built by focusing on what unites, not just what makes us different.
3. **Lead Like a Conductor:** Leaders should know when to highlight individual voices and when to step back and let others lead.
4. **Use People's Strengths:** Delegating based on gifts and energy—not just roles—builds momentum, trust, and shared ownership.

3 Questions for Your Team

1. In what ways are we appreciating and leveraging different perspectives and voices on our teams?
2. How well do you know the strengths of the people you lead?
3. What are you doing to build belonging on your team?

7

Scholarship – "Beware Spinning Too Many Plates"

ON JUNE 15, 1958, Erich Brenn took the stage before the cameras of the Ed Sullivan show.[33] Brenn was a plate spinner (aren't we all?). You've seen these acts before, I'm sure. He starts a plate spinning rapidly atop a thin dowel rod. Once it's going, he adds another. And another. Before long, Brenn had thirteen plates spinning at once, and he was frantically moving from one to another, ensuring none of them fell. He can leave some of them alone because they are spinning well, but he must tend to the ones that need him most. Somehow, he stayed calm and collected, moving quickly through the process, and not a single plate fell.

I was always fascinated by this video. Why thirteen? Surely, he could do more. Wouldn't fifteen be even better than thirteen? Then it hit me (not the plate). When the lights are on and the cameras roll, Erich Brenn knows precisely how many plates to spin. Thirteen is exactly the number he can keep going while staying calm and not dropping any. Imagine if he did fourteen and one of them fell. No one would remember the thirteen that stayed up. We would only focus on the one that dropped.

As leaders, we are required to spin plates constantly. But if we spin too many plates, we will get distracted, overscheduled, and stretched too thin. The people we lead will eventually only be able to see the things we drop: the appointments we miss, the messages we don't respond to, and the schedule or meeting changes.

Being a great leader requires discipline and focus. Erich Brenn had the self-discipline to spin thirteen plates on TV. This self-discipline allowed him to stay focused on the task at hand and do a great job, earning him credibility with everyone watching. He was a scholar of his craft.

Leaders who display self-discipline and focus are helpful. Leaders who lack discipline and focus can be damaging. Leaders who know their limits draw people in and toward goals. Leaders who drop plates push people away. Being a scholar of your craft means doing a good job, both as someone who executes tasks and as a leader of people. Becoming a scholar of leadership starts with building self-discipline.

SELF-DISCIPLINE

When you think about the word discipline, what comes to mind? Most people that I talk to about this subject see discipline as a negative word, even though they know more discipline would be useful to us all. When I think of the word discipline as a teacher, I think of office referrals for behavior or inappropriate cell phone usage. As a leader, professional development plans come to mind for struggling teachers.

I would often have this conversation with my students. Being a successful musician requires a great deal of self-discipline. You must set aside time to practice and have a plan for how to practice. You also need to record yourself and listen back so you can hear exactly how things are going. Inevitably, students admit that they want more discipline, but they seem to prefer someone to impose it on them rather than develop self-discipline.

It was always important to remind them, as I remind you now, that everything worthwhile in our lives is uphill. Progress requires work, and work requires discipline. When we begin to take control of our lives and leadership, we understand that self-discipline is not only good for us but is often required for us to grow.

Let's look at some best practices for building self-discipline. These work in school, in fitness, at home, and anywhere you are learning to do something better.

Start Small and Build Gradually.

Neither Rome nor self-discipline was built in a day. Both are built over time, a piece at a time, gradually. If you want to get in shape, start with one workout a week. If you're going to learn an instrument, start with one to two notes. If you want to be a great educational leader, give yourself small goals to strive toward. If you want to be more reliable in visiting classrooms, start by blocking your calendar one to two hours at a time and ask someone to hold you accountable to that new schedule.

The key is not to allow distractions to creep in and take over. Self-discipline is about taking control of the results you want. In his book, *Atomic Habits*, James Clear discovered, "If you can get 1% better each day for one year, you'll end up 37 times better by the time you're done."[34]

Set a routine or schedule.

There is no substitute for the power of habit, routine, and schedule. People who lack both are unpredictable and hard to follow. One routine I have for myself is to put my workout clothes beside the bed each night. That way, when my alarm goes off at 5 a.m., I have one less excuse to stay in bed. That routine encourages me to get up and go.

One school routine that worked for me was to have a five-minute countdown displayed on our projector after the bell rang to start class. This told everyone exactly when we were going to start. It gave the students time to get their instruments and find their seats, and it gave me a deadline to stay focused and manage my time well. The countdown clock was a major part of our class culture. Sometimes I had to end conversations abruptly when the timer ran low, but it kept us all on track.

Eliminate Distractions.

This is a big one because, as an educational leader, you are surrounded by distractions. Managing them and keeping your priorities straight is a big deal. One big distraction is likely in your pocket right now—your phone. We are tethered to them, aren't we? Dr. Elmore likes to say, "When our phones had leashes (cords), we were free. Now our phones are free, and we have leashes."

How can we control this big distraction?

At the beginning of my classes, I would often take my phone out and show it to the students. Early in the semester, I would tell them, "Nothing you do today will be as interesting to me as these dumb notifications on my phone. It's just how we are wired." I would then place my phone face down on the desk in front of me and ask them to do the same. We all knew and agreed that this was necessary to control the distractions of all the notifications we received each day.

Sometimes, I would be even more honest with my students and tell them I could give them an hour break from whatever demands their parents or significant others might place upon them via text or email (they always nodded in agreement). They were free to blame me for not being able to text back. I would do the same if someone texted me. In those moments, we built discipline together.

Surround Yourself with Support

It's hard to build discipline on your own. Who is holding you accountable for your goals? You've heard the phrase, "It's lonely at the top." Leaders need mentors, too. Surround yourself with supportive people, communicate your goals, and have regular check-ins with them on your progress.

Even in places with an "I LOVE THIS PLACE" culture, there will be hard times and heavy periods of distraction and stress. Well-built systems of self-discipline can withstand even the most challenging situations.

Whenever my students would complain about something being difficult, taking too long, or the process of becoming a scholar becoming boring, I would remind them, "You can have the pain of discipline now or the pain of regret later." It's a powerful quote to help us remember that without discipline, we may feel good now, but later things may get much worse.

As you build self-discipline and help the people you lead do the same, I wanted to share some strategies that I have learned from leaders who have guided me and my colleagues over the years. As you read through the list, consider one, two, or ten of them and think about how you could implement them at your place. It will take discipline, but these are ways to build credibility and confidence with those you lead.

10 TIME-TESTED PRINCIPLES FROM SCHOOL LEADERS

1. Visit classrooms more.

More classroom visits will lower the tension teachers often feel when their leadership enters the classroom. Aim for less assessment and more "checking in". As a teacher, it's always lovely to have leadership come by just to see how things are going and give a pat on the back in a "non-evaluative" environment. It's also great practice for teachers to visit each other's classrooms, if for nothing else than to support one another and observe a colleague doing good work!

2. Establish norms.

Establishing a shared vision and expectations for all is crucial. Teachers want to hear from their leaders about the evaluation processes, but they also need a vision for how quality instruction can be delivered and shared in the building.

Students want to hear what levels of structure and expectations their teacher has for them. Brene Brown says, "unclear is unkind."[35] Be clear about norms and expectations.

3. **Give specific feedback.**

Everyone wants to be told "great job." However, we also want to grow and know that our leaders see potential in us. A leader who can pinpoint a part of a lesson that can be improved in a practical and specific way will earn the respect of those they lead. It also helps to show that they were paying close attention to what was happening in the lesson. Our students may not admit it, but they want our feedback as well. Being specific about what they can improve upon will help them to grow and show you care about them individually.

4. **Ask Great Questions**

I once heard, "You can tell how much knowledge someone has by what they say. But you can tell how wise they are by what questions they ask." A leader who asks questions seems genuinely interested in the person they're leading, and that builds trust and respect. Remember to be both tough AND tender.

5. Model expectations.

Effective leaders lead by example and do not ask teachers or students to do anything they wouldn't do themselves, especially regarding technology integration, evaluations, and improving pedagogical practice. A tough and tender leader is someone who knows the way, shows them the way, and **goes** the way.

6. Prioritize growth.

Attend at least one conference or workshop a year that aligns with a significant school or district initiative. Read one education book and one from another field, such as general leadership strategies or self-help.

Consider allowing teachers to choose their professional development opportunities. Encouraging them to pursue their professional growth will cultivate a scholarly mindset.

This principle holds in classrooms as well. Student choice and student voice are major components of a healthy twenty-first century classroom. Allowing students to choose their learning opportunities helps us to build influence with them.

7. Teach a class.

Earlier, I mentioned that school leaders can often seem to have forgotten what it's like to teach. Take the place of a substitute teacher or step in for a teacher who may need a break—or just do it for fun! Modeling good pedagogy and going "back to your roots" will go a long way to building culture and trust with those you lead. Teachers, invite your administrators in to observe and then involve them in the learning process!

8. Make reflection a regular practice.

My principal, Mrs. Stewart, was a master at reflecting on her leadership. Our reflections aid our personal growth and catalyze others to reflect on their practice to develop professionally. She encouraged teachers to write brief reflections before post-conferences to foster a more collaborative conversation on improvement.

9. Co-observe.

Collaborate with members of your team to co-observe lessons. This allows for different perspectives and varied expertise, as well as opportunities to improve pedagogical leadership skills and reflect on observations. The same goes for us as teachers. If we have common planning periods with our collaborative team or PLC's, consider using those as opportunities to observe a colleague.

10. Utilize Coaching Strategies

Coaching is about asking questions, not about giving advice. This approach allows you to help the teacher or student unlock their potential using what they already know and will enable you to help them grow without having a working knowledge of their content area.

It's easy to assume that your learning journey is finished once you become a school leader. Tough and tender leaders know better! As legendary basketball coach John Wooden once said, "It's what you learn after you know it all that counts!"[36] Coach is spot on. Once we are well educated, experienced, and have the influence to match, we can still learn and grow as scholars.

While I love this list of strategies to build discipline as a school leader, self-discipline is only part of the journey to becoming a scholar. The purpose of discipline is to put it into practice in the areas that are most useful in leading others. As we consider scholarship a major component of our tough and tender leadership, we must also see how it pairs with focus. Let's start by discussing focus with one of my favorite historical examples of how it can make or break our leadership goals. Meet Robert and Roald.

THE RACE TO THE SOUTH POLE[37]

By 1910, humanity had few undiscovered lands. Since American explorer Robert Peary reached the North Pole in 1909, explorers like Robert Falcon Scott and Roald Amundsen saw the South Pole as the final grand prize.

Sir Robert Falcon Scott was a British Royal Navy officer and famed explorer. He had already visited Antarctica on a previous expedition, setting a record for the furthest south ever traveled and discovering the Antarctic Plateau on which the South Pole is located.

Roald Amundsen was a Norwegian explorer who, in 1903, became the first to sail the Northwest Passage above Canada, connecting the Atlantic and Pacific Oceans. Amundsen had also visited Antarctica previously as first mate on an expedition in 1897. Both men knew the South Pole hadn't been touched and vowed to be the first to reach it.

Scott's expedition to the South Pole left Britain on June 15, 1910, aboard his ship, the *Terra Nova* (*New Land*), cheered on by throngs of British patriots excited to see their country on the move again. On board, Scott had sixty-five crew, horses, dogs, sleds, food rations, supplies, fuel, and three state-of-the-art motorized sleds, the predecessor to the snowmobile. Scott's expedition was well-known and well-funded.

Amundsen also left in June of 1910 on his ship, the *Fram* (*Onward*); however, the similarities between the two end there. His team of nineteen men and 100 sled dogs set sail under the cover of darkness. There were no ponies or motorized sleds, and very little funding. Indeed, Amundsen traveled light by comparison, bringing only what he thought he needed to get the job done.

On paper, this was not a fair fight. Scott had a clear advantage in terms of workforce and resources.

Fast forward to January 17, 1912. Robert Falcon Scott and four other men finally reached the South Pole, having made the nearly 1,800-mile journey from the *Terra Nova*, taking just over one year to do so. Freezing and almost starving, the scene that met Scott at the pole was sure to take his breath away.

That scene, unfortunately, included a Norwegian Flag. It had been placed there by Roald Amundsen thirty-five days earlier. The smaller, less resourced Norwegian party had bested their British counterparts by five weeks! Amundsen was a third of the way back to his ship by the time Scott arrived at the pole.

Both men had accomplished what they set out to do, but Roald Amundsen was the clear winner if the goal was to be the first one to the South Pole. Amundsen's team demonstrated a key characteristic that every great leader must develop to be a scholar of their craft: **FOCUS.**

By analyzing the two expeditions and their objectives, we can learn a valuable lesson about how focus affects leaders.

LESSONS FROM THE RACE

Robert Falcon Scott had four objectives, not one. Because his investors had given so much money to this venture, they felt they had a stake in his decisions while there (It's their equivalent of the "I pay my taxes and thus your salary" email.). In particular, the Royal Geographical Society entrusted Scott with at least three additional goals (see #2 below).

Scott's Objectives:

1. Reach the South Pole First
2. Scientific Exploration
3. Technological Innovation
4. Rekindle British Pride[38]

Scott knew his expedition would be publicly judged based on whether he got to the pole first. This was priority number one. However, since his backing came mainly from the science community, he traveled with multiple teams interested in fields like Glaciology, Geology, Cartography, Zoology, Botany, and Meteorology.

In technological innovation, Scott spent more money on three prototype motorized sleds than Amundsen did on his entire expedition! Of course, he felt pressure to use them. And they were a disaster. One fell off the ship during unloading and sank straight to the bottom (expensive oops), while the others proved they could not function in such cold conditions. Despite all the expertise onboard, Scott did not employ a single mechanic capable of motorized sled repair.

Finally, in the years leading up to the expedition, many British (men) felt that the national pride they had once felt in their youth had waned. Scott had been entrusted not only with being first to the pole but also with doing things "the British way." This meant the hard way. So, for much of the 1,800-mile journey, Scott's men pulled their sleds across the Antarctic terrain themselves.

The sad truth is that Robert Falcon Scott lost nearly every member of his traveling party, including his own life. On March 29, 1912, his final party of five perished a mere eleven miles from an aid station nearby. They could not make it to safety through a blizzard that had cropped up days before.

Let's turn to Amundsen. Not only did he reach the pole first, but not a single human life was lost in the process. You see, Amundsen had one focus, and it drove his mission. Before departing, he wrote:

"Our plan is one, one, and again one alone—to reach the pole. For that goal, I have decided to throw everything else aside. We shall do what we can without colliding with this plan."[39]

As leaders, we can easily fall prey to the same lack of focus that doomed the Scott expedition. Our teams will stick together if we develop ourselves as leaders with focus. The stakes may not be so high that people will perish, but if the mission is not our sole focus and our discipline is not strong enough to help us get there, everyone around us will suffer.

I LOVE THIS PLACE culture requires leaders to focus on a better future for everyone and the discipline to eliminate anything that might distract them from achieving it. Using the chart below, let's look at the difference between focused and unfocused leaders:

An Unfocused Leader	**A Focused Leader**
Constantly Distracted	Eliminates Distraction
Says YES A Lot	Says NO a Lot
Unscheduled and Aware	Keeps A Calendar and Commitments
Everything Is an Emergency	Manages Priorities Well
Does Everything Themselves	Delegates Tasks to Others
Is Unavailable and Inaccessible	Is Present and Approachable

As you consider the table, some names likely appear in your mind in both columns. Perhaps you stopped on one or two items and thought, "I need to do better here." That's good! You don't have to have this mastered yet. We are just raising our awareness level about our focus.

As an educational leader, some of my chief frustrations with our fellow leaders are related to this area. A leader who is neither present nor approachable is tough to follow. A leader who cancels appointments or continually changes observation times is frustrating to work for. A leader who is distracted or overscheduled (or both) is of little value to the team.

We must ask ourselves some tough questions in order to be available for our team:

1. Is my calendar too full to connect with the people I am leading?
2. What problems need solving now versus what can wait until later?
3. Am I too busy to stay calm in the face of challenges?
4. What can I delegate to other team members?
5. Am I approachable and available?

We can do anything, but we cannot do everything. For teachers, it is very empowering when their school leaders ask them to take on an important task. It says, "I trust you." As scholars of leadership, it is our job to cultivate and model self-discipline and focus. We may often think this is a complicated task, but it is not. There is one big way we can gain influence over the people we lead, and that is by doing our jobs well.

FOCUSED SCHOOL LEADERSHIP

I recently had a conversation with my friend Amber about this topic. She is a new principal at a local elementary school and had some wonderful things to say about staying focused. She told me her job sometimes feels like a circus act. Imagine juggling hiring, curriculum, facilities, athletics, and the occasional "apple in the toilet" emergency (Yes, that actually happened.). However, Amber's key is to remain calm in the middle of all of it. She self-identifies as a "laid-back principal."

Her team has a weekly ritual called the "barometer meeting." In it, they ask each other three important questions about their teams: "Are we safe? Are we connected? Are we thriving?" If not, they determine what needs to be adjusted and try to eliminate anything that doesn't make the teachers' lives easier.

She's also worked to ditch time-wasting meetings, because who really needs another hour-long PowerPoint presentation? She told me about some teachers who sat through a long meeting but only needed to be present for the first five to ten minutes. They worked together with the person in charge of those meetings and made a plan that respected the time of the people who didn't need to be present for the whole meeting.

She's also made efforts to be as visible as possible. Every morning, she and her fellow admin team appear on the school news, making jokes and showing kids and staff that they are approachable. She's also in the hallways, leaving little notes for students. She had a custom stamp made that tells students she loves their work, so they know she saw it even if they weren't there at the time. Her philosophy? Be visible, be human, and don't be afraid to laugh at yourself.

She told me about one blazing hot staff meeting, and Amber couldn't stop fussing with her hair. She told everyone, "Sorry, I'm cranky because it's so hot, and I can't find a hair tie." Later, she walked into her office to find her desk covered in hair ties. Her team's little prank showed just how much they appreciated her authenticity—and her sense of humor. I think this could only happen to a leader who is focused, approachable, and visible in their building.

Amber's story is a great illustration of focused leadership. She doesn't try to spin every plate herself. Instead, she builds trust, keeps her priorities clear, and always remembers to have a little fun. After all, leading a school isn't just about keeping the plates spinning—it's about knowing which ones are worth spinning in the first place.

THE 1-4-3 – CHAPTER 7: SCHOLARSHIP – "BEWARE SPINNING TOO MANY PLATES"

1 Quotable Quote

"We can do anything, but we cannot do everything."

You can't lead well if you're chasing every task and dropping the ones that matter most. Discipline and focus aren't extras—they're essentials.

4 Key Takeaways

1. **Don't Spin Too Many Plates:** Doing too many things at once leads to mistakes, missed opportunities, and burnout—for both leaders and teams.
2. **Scholarship Requires Discipline:** Great leaders are students of their craft, building consistent habits and routines to grow.
3. **Focus Builds Influence:** The most effective leaders know what to say yes to—and what to say no to.
4. **Presence Matters:** A leader's visibility, clarity, and availability are essential to building trust and maintaining a healthy culture.

3 Questions for Your Team

1. What's one plate you need to stop spinning so you can focus on what matters most?
2. How are you modeling discipline and focus to those you lead?
3. If your students or staff followed your lead when it came to your time, energy, and follow-through, what would that look like?

8

Trust = "Gratitude + Growth"

ONE OF THE toughest and most tender leaders I ever worked with was Sherri Thoroughman. Sherri was an English teacher turned assistant principal who was also our athletic director (AD). Something you should know: the AD and the band director must get along. The marching band may not be an official sports team, but our students attend all football games, home and away, play at pep rallies, and sometimes they even do in-building parades for teams that make the playoffs.

There are a lot of moving parts when we travel to those away games. Our organization traveled on five buses, bringing along a fifty-four-foot semi-trailer, a sixteen-foot pull-behind trailer, and often a twenty-four-foot box truck. We brought along an army of chaperones and equipment crew, all of whom required entry to the game. The AD had the power to make all those logistics easy (or difficult) for us.

Sherri was also my evaluator for a time, and it was a regular occurrence to see her in the band room to watch. She was one of a few administrators who would come by "just to escape from the rest of the school." Seeing the kids make music was fun for her.

She was also the first to admit she knew nothing of what we did. She thought it was magic. She could often be seen talking to kids about what they were doing or asking them to wear a drum or a sousaphone (marching tuba) so she could see how heavy they were. She always showed a real appreciation for what kids were being asked to do both outdoors and indoors.

That level of gratitude went a long way when it came to evaluation time. Sherri walked us through some difficult times and conversations. One year, we had a particularly challenging booster club, and she would come to the meetings to verify that everything was above board. Then, she and I would meet, and she would remind me of things I needed to do to keep the organization on track. They were hard conversations navigating hard times.

Another time, I had just hired a young teacher to serve as our assistant director. She was (and still is) an incredibly talented teacher, and the students loved her. However, she and I struggled to see eye to eye at first—call it "generational differences." On numerous occasions, Sherri called me out privately for not doing enough to foster a connection. My right to correct my fellow teacher was only valid if I had done the work to connect.

We were able to have those difficult conversations because Sherri had been present. She had an outward appreciation for what we were doing, even though she admitted to not understanding it. She was a coach, not a musician, but that never stood in her way of connecting first and correcting second.

Leading people is always challenging. School leaders are often former teachers in charge of current teachers. They must evaluate, guide, and coach them toward a common goal. The good ones, like Sherri Thoroughman, usually get one thing right. They build trust by balancing gratitude and growth.

Showing gratitude creates a personal connection. It reminds us that we are leading people, not problems. Fostering connection also enables us to give corrections that will be received well. Correction before connection is the wrong order of operations.

However, leading people also requires helping them grow. Growth usually involves a direct challenge to improve in some area (professionally or personally). Giving feedback is essential to someone's growth and development. We help them see that responding well to failure is often the only way forward. We teach them that overcoming obstacles is the way to do better. All this requires understanding how emotional bank accounts work.

OUR EMOTIONAL BANK ACCOUNTS

Perhaps you've heard of John Gottman? Gottman is a psychologist, researcher, and Professor Emeritus at the University of Washington. Most of his career has been spent studying long-term relationships, mostly marriage, looking for ways to predict (and prevent) divorce (If 40 percent of marriages end in divorce, then 60 percent end in death. Uplifting fact of the day.).

Of the fascinating findings in Gottman's work, my favorite is the 5:1 "magic ratio." The magic ratio says that every lasting and trusting relationship should have five positive interactions for every negative interaction. Simply put, conflict is inevitable and must be intentionally balanced with encouragement.[40] **This is how we build trust.**

Gottman also found that if the positive-negative ratio during periods of conflict is 1:1 or less, the relationship is bound to end poorly. **This is how we destroy trust.**

Now, no one has time to consider their emotional scorecard with everyone, ensuring the ratio is sustained. People in lasting relationships don't do that, and people in strained ones don't either (Though they are much more likely to "keep score," aren't they?). Keeping score isn't the point.

The 5:1 ratio is like an emotional bank account. Withdrawals are made in increments of five, while deposits are made in singles. We must make more deposits than withdrawals to prevent the account from going bankrupt.

This metaphor reminds us that every time we encourage someone and care about them, we make a deposit into that account. When we correct them and directly challenge them to improve, we withdraw from the account. Even if we give feedback very well, it is often felt as a withdrawal by the receiver. Understanding the process of withdrawals and deposits enhances our influence and builds trust.

Think of it this way. **We leave no one behind because we care about them and are grateful they're on our team. We leave no one where we found them because we know they need to grow.** We can help them succeed with appropriate feedback and coaching.

Sherri Thoroughman knew the formula for building trust. She put change in my account, allowing her to correct me without losing the relationship. She intentionally connected with me, my staff, and our students so that when the need for correction arose, the relationship wasn't lost. The formula for building trust in the people you lead involves gratitude and growth.

There's one more very important thing. **If you're giving feedback out of frustration, you've waited too long to give it.** We often let things go or slide to maintain the relationship or avoid hurting someone's feelings (think back to cotton candy leadership). But that isn't sustainable because we aren't investing in that person's growth. We are leaving them behind.

Eventually, if that person doesn't grow or someone else doesn't step in to coach them, they will be too far behind to ignore them any further. And when they are that far behind, we must either turn back or slow down to get them or turn around and yell at them to catch up. That frustration harms the relationship.

Leaders who build trust well give feedback early and often and balance that feedback with positivity and encouragement. That's the way forward.

Remember, holding people accountable is a form of compassion. It says I care enough to neither leave you behind nor leave you where you are. Let's explore how to put all this into practice with two areas that I believe all schools should grow: how we recognize people and how we give them feedback.

RECOGNITION IS GRATITUDE IN ACTION

One of the overlooked aspects of leadership, especially in education, is recognition. Some schools do this better than others, but I have long believed we can do much better to make teachers, students, and other staff feel appreciated.

Recognition is the physical manifestation of gratitude. Here are six meaningful ways to recognize our people.

Vocal Praise

This is the easiest and cheapest. Vocal praise costs nothing and pays great dividends. In a BambooHR study of various workplaces, 94 percent of employees who received positive recognition regularly rated themselves "very happy" with their jobs.[41] Giving praise on an individual and personal level is a great investment.

Giving praise to a teacher in front of their students is a big deal. It could be as simple as a principal or assistant principal being in a classroom, observing what's going on, and simply saying, "You are doing a great job. Students, you are very lucky to have this teacher." The "street cred" that comes with it will generate an amazing amount of connection and trust. As suggested in the previous chapter, visiting more classrooms (without an agenda other than praise) allows this practice to occur regularly.

One word of caution, however. A wise teacher once told me to avoid giving false praise for a job well done. It is often a knee-jerk reaction when someone is trying to do something to say to them, "Good job." What we usually mean is "good effort." Confusing the two can be harmful.

At best, the person knows it was NOT a good job and shrugs off your comment as an attempt to be kind. At worst, the person believes you, thinks they have done enough, and stops growing.

Here's a helpful adage to carry with you:

> "When effort is high, and success is low. Praise the effort."
>
> "When effort is high, and success is high. Praise the success."
>
> "When neither is high, ask good questions."

In the latter situation, instead of trying to fix it, ask, "How can I help you with this?" "What is standing in the way of your success here?" or "What do you need from me to accomplish your goals?"

When I was getting my leadership certificate from Berry College, I took a coaching class. Part of that class was to coach a colleague, and so I asked our chorus teacher if I could coach her since she was a new teacher. She agreed. Throughout several meetings, I sat with her and simply asked questions. "What area do you want to grow?" "What practices could you put into place to grow in that area?" "How can I support you in this?" It was a great season for us both, and I think she was surprised at how many questions I asked and how little advice I gave.

Leading with questions opens the dialogue for the person you are coaching to take the lead. It's believing that they have the tools and the willpower to grow themselves; you simply help them unlock it.

Perhaps they are stressed about something unrelated to their job and need time to cope or reflect. Maybe they completely misunderstood the assignment. Or possibly they aren't sure what they need and ask for your support. In every case, you, as a leader, have won influence and trust.

Never underestimate the power of vocal praise. Let's move on.

Experiences

People love to do things. They love to do things with people they love even more. Host a family tailgate at a football game (provide free food!). Honor those with spouses or significant others by sponsoring a date night. A high school (or middle school) could even offer free student-led babysitting services so the adults could enjoy a night out. Provide tickets to school events and games for teachers to enjoy the fruits of student efforts in the arts and athletics.

Experiences could also be professional learning (PL) opportunities. Send your teachers to conferences, workshops, or conventions that interest them. When I was teaching, my principals always encouraged us to attend our state music educators' convention to learn, grow, and network. They would even let us out of final exam week to attend our annual international convention in Chicago.

They openly admitted that they couldn't provide us with great professional learning opportunities for music and instead encouraged us to pursue our own. "Time away" that doesn't impact sick or personal leave was like oxygen to our souls. We always came back feeling refreshed.

My friend Andy is a master of providing professional experiences. He was a middle and high school principal for years, having since retired. He always took groups of his teachers on PL trips out of state. He strongly acknowledged the need to get away from the building, away from the distractions of home, and away from the state to see what else was happening in the world of education.

His goal in these trips was twofold. First, he wanted his teachers to see everything they were doing **right** in their building. It was a trip of encouragement.

Second, he wanted to **build relationships** with his teacher-leaders. He allowed them to choose what they wanted to do in their spare time. On one trip, they went to Disneyland. Another time, they explored the surrounding areas, looking for fun shops or exciting things to do. The crucial component was that they were building relationships and sharing experiences. He wanted them to be together, not holed up in their hotel rooms. Those teachers returned to school recharged, shouting praises over their school and their leader. That's major trust-building.

If not a trip, bring in dynamic and engaging professional learning presenters if trips. Shameless plug: We have some great ones at Growing Leaders and Maxwell Leadership! Ask your staff what they want to learn and find an expert to bring it to them!

Freedom

You lead adults. What freedoms and independence can you offer them? Is there any flexibility in their start and end times? Are teachers allowed to leave during planning to run errands, get lunch, or care for their needs without having to "spend the saved time?"

In my experience, the norm in education seems to be taking away time and rarely giving it back. There's always some lunch and learn, planning-time meeting, or new tardy or lunch duty that sets us back. Of course, these may be necessary, but what would giving time look like? What flexibility can you offer to the adults you lead?

You may be thinking, Patrick, "What if they abuse it?" My response? "**What if they don't?**" What if they **use** it? What if they're happier because they can plan, take care of their business, and feel like the professional adults they are?

You can do this without being overt. A school leader I once had would get on the intercom during "teacher workdays" after lunch and say, "I'm going to be in my office for the next three hours. This means I won't be able to be in the hallways to check and see if you are working. Do with this as you please." Of course, this was a secret code to let us know that she trusted us to do what we needed to, and if that meant leaving early, so be it.

Giving freedom screams, "I trust you!" And trusting people goes a long way to them saying, "I LOVE THIS PLACE."

Money and Food

It seems silly, but is it possible? Who doesn't love free money, particularly for a job well done? Maybe it's not cash, but gift cards. What flexibility do you have as a leader to reward someone financially? I can't think of a single time that someone offered me money for a job well done, and I responded, "No thanks, I have enough."

One thing I remember really loving was our "Teacher of the Month" program. Each month, a teacher was recognized for their hard work and received a $50 gift card to a local restaurant. The person who won was always encouraged to make time for a date night with their significant other or spouse (or a friend). No one ever complained about getting a free meal!

My wife and I worked in the same building for eight years before I took a new job. We would always nominate each other for Teacher of the Month because if one of us won, we both won!

Or perhaps money isn't in the budget. What about food? If we can't fill bank accounts, at least we can fill stomachs. Our administration at Hillgrove always provided snacks and treats at extra meetings, which helped.

Another way that we recognized students with food was Performance Evaluation Cake Day. Performance evaluation was like our state standards evaluation. It's a big deal for all the performing groups in the state, and we typically spend two to three months preparing for the concert.

Those performances usually happened on Thursday and Friday, and therefore, Monday was cake day. It was simply a congratulatory party, with cake, to celebrate the student's efforts and successes. We always followed the cake with reflection activities and discussions of the results. But it always started with cake. Because, let's be honest, so many great things start with cake.

Awards

Most schools have some teacher of the month or teacher of the year program, and likely have awards for classified employees (custodians, clerks, paraprofessionals, etc.). However, if the processes behind the awards aren't clear or well-managed, this can be a slippery slope.

Teacher of the Year in our school always felt like a popularity contest (Full disclosure: I was third three times, and I may still be salty about it.). Teachers were nominated by their peers and the faculty voted on who should win.

What always struck me was how often the winner came from a department with a large number of teachers. This makes sense because if you can't win, you want your colleague to win, making your department look good. Poor old fine arts with its eight teachers never stood a chance—seventeen years, never a Fine Arts winner.

Allowing the students to have a say in the teacher of the year might be a good idea. This would lend some credence to the person being a great teacher. Of course, again, I'm biased. (As the band director with over 15 percent of the school in my classes, maybe I could've won.)

I have digressed enough.

One more note about awards is to avoid cheap certificates. A cheap certificate, even hand-signed, conveys no value to the person winning the award. Spend money on plaques, trophies, or even unique awards that say, "You have value enough for us to spend some money on you."

One year, Growing Leaders did something unique that I loved. They gave a "Courageous Leader" award to two adults and a student who made significant contributions. My student Nathan (whom I'll tell you more about later) was the student winner in 2020. The award was a laser-engraved ice-climbing axe. HOW COOL! The logo at the time was a mountain climber, and it fits both the brand and a willingness to show the person how much they matter.

Spend some time and money on your awards, and make sure the criteria for winning are clear.

Rituals, Artifacts, and Gifts

I am a huge fan of rituals. (In a totally non-cult way, you'll see.)

While award ceremonies recognize a few people at specific times, rituals recognize many people much more often. While the award recognizes a person, the ritual recognizes a special moment people shared.

A gift or a meaningful artifact is a great motivator. They aren't voted on; they are earned through commitment and dedication. They can be handmade or bought, but they should be weighty and of good quality to communicate the person's value. If it's apparel, give nice apparel. Spend money and time on it, and perhaps have a committee design it. No one wants more clothes they aren't going to wear.

I have two examples of rituals and artifacts that paid dividends to the people I led over the years (both students and adults). Feel free to steal these ideas or use them as motivation to find your own.

The Nuts-and-Bolts Ritual: Who helps you hold it together?

I borrowed this idea from leadership guru Scott Lang. We used this ritual to celebrate the end of the long journey of a marching band season. The materials needed were one bolt and three nuts for each person (plus extras, of course). I would get them at Home Depot for less than $20.

The ritual was as follows.

1. The bolt is you.
2. The three nuts represent three people who helped you "hold it together" this season.

3. The students and adults were given time to walk around and give one of their nuts to three different people and explain why.

Check the metaphor: Separately, nuts and bolts are worth almost nothing. Together, they hold together buildings, bridges, cars, and planes. Simply put, we are stronger together.

Having someone walk up to you, place a hexagonal nut in your hand, and say, "You were that person to me," is a deeply emotional experience. We always had to be on the lookout for the lonely freshman who maybe only got one or two. Our student leaders always had an extra to give to that person to ensure they felt like they belonged.

At the end of it all, through all the tears and joy, we gave them some cord to tie their fastened nuts and bolts around their neck and proudly wear for everyone to see. This activity took fifteen minutes, but the emotional bank account investment paid dividends for months and years. I still have all mine, and you can often see students still wearing theirs. My oldest son has four sets hanging from his rear-view mirror.

The best part? It was a ritual that involved every single person with an artifact that rewarded their efforts. It let them know they mattered to their peers.

The Challenge Coin Ritual: A unique reward for finishing the job.

There are several origin stories of the challenge coin. This one's my favorite.[42]

During World War I, many men volunteered as the US began to build up its Army Air Corps. One of those men was a wealthy lieutenant who wanted to give each member of his unit a memento, so he ordered several coin-sized bronze medallions to be made featuring their unit's insignia.

The lieutenant put his medallion in a small leather pouch around his neck.

A short time later, his plane was shot down over Germany. He survived but was captured by a German patrol. They took all his personal effects, so he would have no way to identify himself if he escaped. For some reason, he was allowed to keep the pouch with the coin inside.

The lieutenant was taken to a small town near the front lines of the war. Despite his lack of ID, he found some civilian clothing and escaped, eventually stumbling into a French outpost. Wary of anyone not in uniform, the French soldiers didn't recognize his accent and immediately assumed he was an enemy.

They planned to execute him since they couldn't ID him. But the lieutenant, remembering he still had the small pouch around his neck, pulled out the coin to show the soldiers his unit's insignia. One of the Frenchmen recognized it, and he was spared.

Instead of being executed, the lieutenant was given a bottle of wine, probably as a form of reparation for his initial treatment. When he finally made it back to his squadron and told the story, it became a tradition for service members to carry a unit-emblazoned coin, just in case.

When I started teaching at Hillgrove, our booster president, Dr. Wizner, suggested rewarding students for surviving the "challenge" of a long, competitive season. Being a brand-new school, we needed some cool traditions, so we jumped on this.

The coin became a part of our culture. I have a case of them at home. Each represents a five-month journey from summer camp to the season's end. We would give them to the students on the last day as a memento, each unique to a "show" they performed in.

From there, we expanded the idea to give coins to students for outstanding musical achievement. When a student did something great, such as making the all-state band, for instance, I would slip a coin into their palm and congratulate them one-on-one in a personal moment. There was no fanfare involved, just genuine gratitude and accomplishment.

Another thing we did was use coins to commemorate special events.

In June 2019, we took over 200 students and parents to Normandy, France, for the seventy-fifth D-Day celebration. As a part of the festivities, we played concerts in the cemeteries at Omaha and Brittany. We decided to have a special "D-Day 75" coin made.

To make the moment more special, each student was given three to five gravestones to find during our time in each cemetery. These were all soldiers from the state of Georgia who lost their lives defending freedom in France. The students found their assigned person and left the challenge coin on the gravestone to thank the soldier who lay there. Many stood silently, some prayed, and others wept, but it was one of the greatest things we ever did.

The coins we bought were made of metal and full of color. They are large and heavy. When placed in your hand, you feel the weight and the craftsmanship. They tell the recipient, "You matter."

Do you have a way to recognize those people that you lead, at a moment's notice, in a personal way? How can you make sure your people know they matter today and in the future? I have long since lost (or tossed) most of the free T-shirts, staff polos, umbrellas, and tumblers we were given over the years. The coins and the nuts and bolts? They sit prominently on my desk.

I love it when an idea catches on. For senior night athletic recognitions, the whole school adopted the coin idea. The principal, AD, and coaches would shake players' hands and put a coin inside them to recognize them for a job well done. It was a great way for our whole school to support recognition in a fun and meaningful way.

Since leaving the classroom, I have brought the coin idea to Growing Leaders. We use them as a thank-you to partners, sliding them into their palms in moments of close connection to show them how much we appreciate being invited to serve their school.

Recognition that communicates gratitude builds trust. Spend the money, time, and creative energy building a culture that takes recognizing people seriously. It's the fast lane to trust, the express lane to "I LOVE THIS PLACE."

Of course, recognition is only part of the battle. We want to reward people for a job well done. But everyone you lead wants to know that growth is on your priority list for them. How we give feedback goes a long way to balance recognition and build trust.

FEEDBACK IS GROWTH FUEL

Have you ever noticed that sometimes feedback comes from unlikely people at unexpected times? I distinctly remember one afternoon getting some firm feedback from a student who sat front and center in my classes for four years. Jayla was an amazing flute player and an incredible human being. She played in our top ensemble starting from her freshman year, a feat reserved for only the most mature young musicians.

During her years in my classes, Jayla earned a great deal of respect from me and her peers by doing a great job, having a reputation for upstanding character, and being a reliable and loving friend. Jayla would also tell you if you needed to improve, as I learned one day after class.

Since Jayla sat so close to me, she got to hear any and all things that I might say under my breath. It was never anything inappropriate, but sometimes, when students do things that are immature or perplexing, we make comments, right? The front row of the band gets to hear many of those asides (most of them directed at the percussion… sigh).

One day, Jayla was packing up to go to lunch. She looked at me and said, "Mr. Erwin, are you aware that you blaspheme a lot?" Now, I knew Jayla was a very spiritual young lady. She usually carried her Bible with her wherever she went, so this was not an out-of-the-ordinary question. But I was taken aback a bit. I didn't think of myself as a blasphemer. I certainly never cursed in front of students!

She said, "Yeah, you say 'Oh my God' under your breath a lot, and you know, that's blasphemy. I think 'Oh my gosh' would be more appropriate for someone of your character." Holy cow! She was right. I did say that a lot. I had to look at Jayla and say, "You're right. I do. I will work on that. Will you help me?" "Of course," she said.

For the next several weeks after that conversation, whenever I got frustrated with someone or something, I would say, "Oh my…" look at Jayla, smile, and end with, "gosh." She would smile back, and we would keep on going.

We have an iLead lesson on giving feedback that uses a metaphor of Surgeons and Vampires. Both vampires and surgeons take blood, and both are a little bit scary when you're a child. Vampires, however, take blood to harm others and heal themselves. Surgeons take blood only to heal the patient. Such is the case with feedback. We can give healing feedback, or we can dole out harmful criticism. The difference is in our intent. Do you want them to grow? Or are you frustrated and just need to feel better?

In the story above, Jayla was a surgeon. She knew what she had to say to me might hurt, but she was doing it for my benefit. She wanted me to grow, and she cared for me. Because she had such a strong reputation as a student and a leader, I was able to hear her words and act on them without any ego at all. She and I were well past the 5:1 ratio.

In my experience giving and receiving both kinds, I developed this helpful chart outlining the difference between harmful criticism and helpful feedback.

Harmful Criticism	Helpful Feedback
Calls Out Mistakes	Calls Out Potential
Is Concerned With The Rules	Is Concerned With the Relationship
Is Generic	Is Specific
Is Delayed	Is Timely
One And Done	Follows Up
One Way Only	Goes Both Ways
Sees The Problem	Sees The Person

Mistakes vs. Potential

We have a saying in music, "Any fool can point out the errors." It doesn't take a leader to tell someone what they did wrong. Great leaders, tough and tender leaders, see the potential in the person and give feedback, leading them to see it for themselves. Use coaching as often as you can, asking guiding questions so the person is led to the conclusion you can already see. And always let them know, "I know you will be able to do this. You just can't do it yet."

In cases like this, sharing stories of when you needed correction and growth is often helpful. We have all struggled, and sharing struggles is a great way to build trust and influence.

Rules vs. Relationships

In discussing Drill Sergeant leadership, I reminded you, "Rules without relationships lead to rebellion."

When delivering feedback, it can be easy to point out a policy that's not correctly followed or missed procedures. Perhaps the person needs further training? Some of our educational procedures can be confusing! Have you ever tried getting buses for a field trip (deep breaths, calm your rage)?

Whatever the situation, try to put the person before the policy. Help them see what needs to be done and give them the necessary scaffolding and resources. Call them, text them, and take the time.

Time spent preparing now is time saved repairing later.

Generic vs. Specific

This is a personal pet peeve of mine. Giving generic feedback is unhelpful, even harmful. Often, this looks like an email or a faculty meeting called to address a procedure that a few teachers aren't following. Does everyone need the reminder, or can you be specific and lead only those who need it?

Blanket statements are also unhelpful. Saying, "Do better," "Try harder," or "You just need to listen," is as unclear as it is useless. We must be specific about what actions need to be taken to correct situations.

Blanket statements tell people you don't trust them and lead to resentment over wasted time and criticism. In my experience, the ones listening already know, and the ones who need the information aren't paying attention anyway!

Whenever possible, be specific about both the action needed and the people who need to take it.

Delayed vs. Timely

Waiting to deliver corrections can be demoralizing to a person. Most people want to know they aren't doing something well sooner rather than later. Perhaps not in front of everyone, we always preached "praise in public, criticize in private." But, if there is feedback to be given, tough and tender leaders use their high level of connection to reach the person and their high standards to teach the person.

Remember, what you allow is what you will get more of. Delaying feedback to avoid difficult conversations isn't helpful for the person you lead. Set up the meeting or send the email sooner rather than later. They will thank you for it in the end.

One-and-Done vs. Following Up

It's a great rule of leadership to correct someone and then follow up to make sure they understand and don't need further support. Too many leaders deliver feedback like a grenade, tossing it into a situation and never coming back to survey the damage. It conveys trust and connection to help someone identify areas for improvement and then check back with them multiple times to ensure they are on the right track. And besides, those check-ins are perfect opportunities to deliver praise and recognition (win-win).

One Way vs. Both Ways

Great leaders see feedback as a two-way street. Don't dish out what you aren't willing to take. When evaluating someone formally or informally, allow them to give you feedback in return. Getting a return investment on your leadership is gold! Someone telling you how you can serve them better improves the culture and working environment.

Besides, we cannot pretend we, as leaders, don't have our flaws. When you ask someone to show them to you, it's often just a reminder that you still need to grow. This trust-building habit of allowing two-way feedback will be a game-changer in connection. Dish it out and take it.

Problems vs. People

In today's educational culture of "fast-paced, get-it-done now, there is no time to waste" teaching and learning, it can be easy to look at all the problems and ignore the people behind them. We do this with student discipline referrals, and we do it with evaluation and feedback. It's too easy to swoop in, fix the problem with a consequence or an action step, and swoop away to the next fire to be put out.

We don't lead problems. We lead people. Building culture requires us to serve people and solve problems together. Will it take more time? Yes. Will it be more difficult? Yes? Is it worth it? I think so.

Remember, to amplify value, the goal is to grow more leaders. If we take the time through connection and feedback to empower others to solve problems for each other, we will build a culture of staying power and resilience. We will be on our way to I LOVE THIS PLACE! But there's one more important lesson. Knowing when to say nothing.

SOMETIMES, SAYING NOTHING IS THE BEST FEEDBACK

Music producer and author Rick Rubin wrote a wonderful book called *The Creative Act*. It is one of the best I've ever read. In it, he reminds us of the physician's oath: "First, Do No Harm." [43]

Every leader should commit to the same oath. We must proceed delicately when giving feedback so as not to do any harm. Rubin delivers a particular bit of wisdom I would like to share here, (paraphrased to fit the purposes of this book):

In the end, the greatest thing a [tough and tender leader] can do is recognize when they have nothing to add. If you are called to give feedback, and truly believe the person is doing well enough to be left alone. Do just that. Saying nothing but "you're doing great, I have nothing to add" is often exactly the step needed. Adding additional input may only serve to water down the results that are already at a high level.

As Rubin says, "Sometimes the most valuable touch a collaborator can have is no touch at all."[44]

THE 1-4-3 – CHAPTER 8: TRUST = "GRATITUDE + GROWTH"

1 Quotable Quote

"We leave no one behind because we care about them. We leave no one where we found them because we know they need to grow."

You can't hold people accountable until they know you care. Trust comes from showing up with gratitude—and staying long enough to help them grow.

4 Key Takeaways

1. **Trust Is Built Daily:** Leaders earn trust by consistently showing appreciation and offering honest, supportive feedback.
2. **Gratitude Comes First:** Recognition—big or small—shows people they matter—connection before correction.
3. **Feedback Fuels Growth:** Accountability is most effective when it's timely, specific, and rooted in care.
4. **Rituals Are Inclusive Forms of Recognition:** Examples like artifacts, symbols, coins, and shared moments make recognition tangible and lasting.

3 Questions for Your Team

1. What's one way you can recognize someone this week that feels personal and specific?
2. Who on your team needs gratitude right now—and who needs growth?
3. What is your typical approach to giving feedback? How can you improve in this area?

9

Leadership – "What Colors Are in Your Box?"

I'M NOT SURE how big high school football is where you live, but in Georgia, it's a big deal. It is such a big deal that more than once in my career, we missed an entire day of school to travel to a playoff game. You see, in the state of Georgia, most of the larger school football powerhouses exist either in the Atlanta area or in the southernmost part of the state. Those two areas are five to six hours apart. When the football team goes to Camden County, Georgia, for a game, five and a half hours hours to our south, the band and cheerleaders go too. And to avoid traffic, we leave at 8 a.m. for a 7:30 p.m. kickoff. Seriously.

I remember the first time we went south for a playoff game; the band and cheerleaders shared two charter buses. When we got to Camden just after lunch, we had time to kill. So, we played games. A favorite was *Heads Up*. Have you ever played the game? It's a great way to pass the time. If you haven't, it's generally played on a mobile device. In the game, the guesser holds a phone on their forehead, and it displays a word, usually part of a category, to make the guessing easier. The other participants then try to get the guesser to say the displayed word by using other related words or acting it out. Watching and playing is usually hilarious.

When we played in Camden, it was the band directors, cheer coaches, and some of our older students all playing together. When one of the cheerleaders had the word "waterbed" on her forehead, one of the cheer coaches, Allerie, started jostling around and making sloshing sounds, and we all lost our minds. I haven't laughed that hard in a long time—good memories with great kids and colleagues.

I love to use a version of this game to teach how our attitude shapes our influence. The guesser holds an "attitude" card on their forehead when we play the game. You can do this with notecards, pre-printed papers, or even a phone. The individual card might say, "I'm happy," "I'm sad," or "I'm proud." The other participants interact with the guesser, acting as if they were giving off that attitude (or vibe, as the kids say).

The game is most fun when played non-verbally. If I held "I'm happy" on my head, others would come to me with thumbs up, smiles, hugs, or high-fives. If I had "I'm angry" up, they might try to calm me down or even avoid me altogether.

The best part about the game is that almost every guesser knows exactly what their "attitude" card says. When we key in on how others act and react in our presence, it's easy to get a feel for the attitude we are giving off.

It makes sense. How do you react if you're around someone who is nearly always angry, frustrated, or generally negative? You likely avoid them or, at best, tolerate their presence. You certainly aren't volunteering to be on their committee or to give them extra support unless you are close and understand the source of their attitude (and even then, perhaps second-guessing it).

The opposite is also true. When someone gives off positive vibes and their attitude is welcoming, encouraging, supportive, and/or happy, you want to spend time with that person. You want to be led by that person. You admire them, even for their ability to stay positive during a storm.

The punch line is the best part about this attitude version of "heads up." We get to **choose** what's on our attitude cards every minute of every day. When we are disciplined with our thoughts and have a handle on our feelings, we can give off whatever vibe we want, even on the hard days.

One of my favorite leaders of all time, Dr. Tim Lautzenheiser, taught me when I was sixteen years old: "You control your thoughts. Your thoughts control your feelings.

Therefore, you control your feelings." Great leaders understand the power of attitude, choose a good one, and use it to influence others.

HABITS AND ATTITUDES

When I started at Growing Leaders, our curriculum was called Habitudes (it's called iLead now). Using it to impact my students was one of the greatest accomplishments of my career. The word Habitude is a combination of habits and attitudes, and there's no better way to describe how to become a leader. We must be in control of both our habits and our attitudes and use them to influence our teams.

Now, there are too many great books about habits for me to write another one. I recommend *The Power of Habit* by Charles Duhigg and *Atomic Habits* by James Clear. Those wonderful works informed me of the power habits have over my life. I would like to point out one major tenet that habits have in terms of our leadership, and that is:

Your Habits Determine Your Future

Habits are built on discipline (see the previous chapter), and discipline, not our desire, determines our destination. American philosopher and psychologist William James said it well when he wrote:

"All our life, so far as it has definite form, is but a mass of habits—practical, emotional, and intellectual—systematically organized for our weal or woe, and bearing us irresistibly toward our destiny, whatever the latter may be."[45]

Another way I liked to describe this principle to students was, "Just because you stand in the garage doesn't make you a car." We must take our desires and put them into action, developing habits that help us grow toward a more desirable future. Habits are a big deal. However, we cannot underestimate the importance of attitude, which leads me to a second point:

Your Attitude Determines Who Will Join You In Your Future

Yes, your habits determine your future destination, whether good or bad. But who will be standing beside you when you get there? Your attitude determines that. Are you someone others want to be around, work for, or follow?

You remember, earlier in the book, I realized that the culture of our program was not causing students to join or stay. My leadership habits and attitudes were creating a future for my organization that didn't include as many students joining me as I wanted. I had to consider how my leadership attitude was affecting the people around me. It was how I was painting the world around me that needed to change.

WHAT COLORS ARE IN YOUR BOX?

One of my favorite quotes that describes the importance of attitude is from Allen Klein, author of a lovely book entitled *You Can't Ruin My Day*, Klein writes:

> Attitude is a box of crayons you use to color your world. Choose grey, and everything will be grey. Try some bright colors and see what happens.[46]

In the latter part of my classroom teaching career, I decided to get very specific about the person I wanted to be for the people I was leading. While determining the tone I wanted to set for our organization, I wrote down six words that describe how I wanted my students and staff to see me. They may not know these words, but when I say them, I hope they will say, "Yeah, that's Mr. Erwin."

Those six words are: "Humorous, Tenacious, Sensitive, Urgent, Encouraging, Listener." Those are the colors I chose for my crayon box.

Humor

They say laughter is the best medicine. Speaking about their book *Humor, Seriously*, Stanford Graduate School of Business faculty members Jennifer Aaker and Naomi Bagdonas say that the return on investment of humor is incredible:

> Leaders with a sense of humor—any sense of humor, not even a good sense of humor—are 27 percent more motivating and inspiring. Their employees are 15 percent more engaged when they work with them. And their teams are twice as creative as measured by having them solve a creativity challenge[47] (Permission to tell Dad Jokes engaged.).

I like to laugh, but I recently realized it's not about being funny. Humor is about being human and connecting with the people you work with and who work for you. Understanding the role humor can play with the people you lead is a great way to be contagious. I tell teachers all the time, "If students are laughing, they are listening."

Laughter also mixes a wonderful cocktail of brain chemicals that bring people together. Laughing together increases dopamine and oxytocin levels and decreases cortisol (fight-or-flight) levels. By laughing together, we develop connections faster and build trust more quickly.

You may wonder, what happens when humor backfires and someone's feelings get hurt? It can happen—it will happen—but it's also an opportunity to connect and correct yourself. I've experienced this a few times, the most memorable being with a student, Hannah.

One day at a marching band rehearsal, a young man showed up with flowers to ask her to the homecoming dance. Prom-posals are a big thing these days. Kids are creative in asking each other out these days. Hannah was clearly embarrassed by the attention, but she said yes (Slay, Hannah.).

The next day, we were practicing indoors, and Hannah said something sassy to me. I quipped back, "Oh, so you get asked to homecoming, and now you can say whatever you want to me?" It was supposed to be funny. I've made jokes like that with her before, and it was fine. But this time, it just brought back the embarrassment she felt when she was asked in public. Hannah didn't speak to me for two days.

I knew I had messed up, so the following week in rehearsal (Hannah actively ignoring me), I asked Bella, who was standing next to her, "Would you please tell Hannah that I'm sorry for what I said? That was wrong of me, and I will never do it again." Hannah smiled and broke her vow of silence, giving me a big hug.

After that moment, our relationship strengthened. Although my attempt at humor may have messed it up, the opportunity to connect with her and correct myself strengthened our relationship (I had to couple my humor with an attitude of humility.).

What I learned about humor at that moment is that it is best reserved for making fun of yourself rather than others. Nine times out of ten, the joke I made toward Hannah would have been funny. The tenth time, it was not. From then on, most of my humor was directed at myself. It can be really humanizing when a leader pokes fun at their flaws.

Tenacious and Urgent

Tenacious and urgent describe my way of operating very well. Remember, our motto was HUSTLE. One way to describe this is the phrase, "The speed of the leader is the speed of the team."

It was my job to set the pace and tempo of my organization. That is not to say we should outpace the team. Leaders can do that if they aren't aware of what their people need. It just means we need to work as hard as we can, for the time that we have, without burning out.

I'm a finisher. I'm tenacious (it's in my working genius). I wanted that to be contagious to others, within their abilities. As the leader, I set the tone. When a sense of urgency needs to be created, the leader must foster that. And, of course, a dose of humor in the process won't hurt.

Encouraging

It is essential for a leader to be encouraging to their people. Hearing "you've got this," "you can do hard things," or "I've got your back" is a tone worthy of setting in every organization.

One of the ways I did this at school was to be at the door, greeting everyone as they came in. I was positive, loud, and high fiving everyone (even those not in my classes). I wanted them to know that my class would be joyful, fun, and engaging, and that I was genuinely glad they were there. Did everyone love it as much as I did? Not a chance. But what choice do we have? If I'm going to get any positive feedback, I need to be an encourager.

In fact, I went to work every day assuming that I was the only positive adult those students would see that day. I didn't know the quality of my students' relationships with their parents, peers, or other teachers, but I could control the quality of their relationships with me.

When I came across staff members or leaders in my building, I had no idea what kind of day they were having. I just assumed they needed me to build them up. It cost me almost nothing, but it paid incredible dividends (I will cover the results in the final section).

Be an encourager. The world needs more leaders like that.

It's just another HUSTLE.

You may groan after reading this, and I'm okay with that. When you take my colors: humor, sensitivity, listening, tenacity, urgency, and encouragement, and rearrange them, it reads like this:

Humor
Urgency
Sensitivity
Tenacity
Listening
Encouragement

(Chicken? Egg? Just go with it)

It's another way that good things come to those who hustle. We become more effective leaders by choosing our attitude. Remember, to hustle is to maximize minutes and moments. These six "attitudes" allow me to do both.

Think of it this way: the people you lead will reflect your attitude and habits, whether you know it or not. You're better off choosing, developing, and sending out the vibes you want from your organization. The best part is you get to choose.

CONTAGIOUS ATTITUDE

Another favorite phrase I would use with students is "As we go, they go. We set the tone." The power of a leader's attitude is in setting the tone and seeing it reflected in those they lead. It's a well-known quote by Tom Stoppard: "A healthy attitude is contagious. Don't wait to catch it from someone else; be a carrier."[48] It is a useful and true maxim for anyone leading others. As we go, they go. Leaders set the tone.

Let's go over some practical ways to ensure our attitude is a healthy one that others can catch.

Model Positivity as Much as Possible

I am an eternal optimist. Students would always ask me, "How are you always so positive?" My simple answer was always "because I choose to be." Was every day great? No way. Did I have struggles? Absolutely. Teaching is hard. But here's a truth I always carried with me:

I don't have the right to share my bad day with an unwilling person.

Of course, there are people in my corner who I need support from and to vent to. My wife would be number one on that list. But in leadership, I can't share my bad days with the people I lead. It's unfair.

Being an optimist, though, doesn't mean I'm not also a realist.

Part of leadership is facing down ugly truths and tough situations. Facing them with realistic optimism, however, is a choice. I can always say, "This is hard, and it's not going to be fun to fix, but I know I can do it, and I'm glad I have help." That's an attitude of leadership. It's a pithy saying, but one I love—the optimist sees the opportunity in every challenge. The pessimist sees the challenge in every opportunity.

You can be an optimist and a realist. They aren't mutually exclusive. In fact, neither is very helpful by itself. When my leadership seemed to be the problem with our recruiting and retention, I had to be a realist and take the blame. I looked at the problem and told myself, "This isn't good, but it's fixable."

It isn't helpful to ignore your problems with only optimism. But it isn't hopeful to look at your problems without any optimism that things can get better. As leaders, we need both.

Mind Your Non-Verbal Signals

I once taught a dear young clarinet player named Kate. Kate sat in the front row (for some reason, all my stories are from the front row), and I had this habit of asking Kate if she was ok. And every day, she would look up and smile and say, "Yes, I'm doing great." One day, Kate came to me and told me she knew why I asked her if she was okay so much. She said, "Mr. Erwin… I have RBF. Resting Bad Face. I'm doing fine; my face doesn't show it."

My wife has a great saying regarding the non-verbal cues we communicate to others. She says don't let yourself get F.A.T.T., and she's not talking about calories. What she means is that leaders must mind their:

Facial Expressions
Actions
Tone
Timing

We've all been talking to someone who is not buying what they are selling. They may be saying the right words, but their face betrays their thoughts. Being mindful of what is on our faces when talking to someone is crucial to being a tough and tender leader.

She also says, "When the actions don't match the words, believe the actions." When we don't do as we say we will, we lose influence. As leaders, we can say all the right things, but following through with those words matters more. Our actions are key non-verbal signals.

Your tone of voice matters as well. It matters more than your words!

Albert Mehrabian, professor of psychology and expert communication researcher, found that the effectiveness of our communication boils down to this:

55 Percent Facial Expression
38 Percent Tone of Voice
7 Percent Word Choice[49]

That's a big deal! You might choose the right words but the wrong tone and body language (fix your face), and your message will be received in a manner you did not expect. We must be mindful of our tone of voice and what it is communicating.

Choosing the right tone is also dependent on the person and situation. This is why the chapter on understanding others came before this one. When considering the "symphony" we lead, some might respond well to loud and gregarious (my specialty), but others will need a gentler touch. Know your people, and this becomes easier.

Encourage and Support Everyone

Remember from the previous chapter that 94 percent of people who feel encouraged and supported at work are satisfied or highly satisfied with their jobs. Encouragement and support cost nothing, but they are incredible tone-setters. Most people just want to be seen, heard, and supported.

Focus on Solutions and Opportunities, not Problems.

It goes without saying that leading in a school setting is fraught with difficulties. You're leading young people, their parents, and highly skilled, often opinionated, adults. There will be problems, and you'll be expected to solve them! The buck stopped with me in the organization I led (hundreds of students, parents, and around a dozen adult staff). I had to be good at solving problems, and many (most) of those problems involved people.

A phrase I learned along the way that helped me solve problems as a good leader was: "People are not problems. Problems are problems." When we see past the person to the problem, we can frame our thoughts regarding solutions and collaboration opportunities. Good luck trying to fix a person.

That's impossible work. Seeing the problem and involving the person in the solution is tough and tender leadership.

You may think, "That person's attitude is the problem!" I hear you. I have dealt with countless students and adults with problematic attitudes. Sometimes, I did a poor job of handling them and wrecked the relationship. Other times, emotional intelligence, attitude, and mindfulness took over, and the relationship grew.

The secret here is to get to know the person and the scenario causing the attitude. As Brene Brown says, "People are hard to hate up close."[50] What is the cause of their attitude? Is it something I am doing or not doing? Is it something at home that is completely unrelated to our current circumstances? Did something happen to them that caused them to lose trust and faith in leaders?

It's hard work, but getting to the root of the problem inside the person is the right work. Have the conversation. Ask the right questions. Connect with them. You might find that the problem is fixable, and they're grateful to be seen and heard.

Approach Your Work with Purpose and Mission

Finally, perhaps most importantly, we must know our purpose and mission. Why do you do what you do (and surely, it's not just for the health benefits)? Do you share both your personal and school mission with the people you lead? This is crucial to being a contagious leader. Do they know your why?

I often shared my mission with my students, and we kept our organizational mission on the wall for them to see daily. I would read it to them sometimes to keep it fresh in their minds. It read:

> We exist to create deliberate success in the lives of our musicians. Each student will strive to be a functionally literate, independent performer who exhibits the highest possible level of leadership and character.

I always felt great about how that reads. Every decision we made fell under that statement. That allowed me, the leader, to positively approach (and even defend) every decision.

When we introduced a leadership development program (which I led once a week, every week) our students asked why we were doing it. I just reminded them of the last phrase of the mission. I wanted to help grow them into people of the highest level of leadership and character.

My friend Ed Morris is a great model for a contagious attitude as a school leader. I mentioned earlier that he was the basketball coach at our school, but these days, he is the head of schools for an excellent local private school. When I asked him about his leadership attitude and what he does, he responded, "I make the coffee."

I pushed him on what that meant, and he said that his school has a faculty gathering area where teachers always go in the morning. They check their mail, pick up copies that may have been made, and check if there is coffee. If you're a coffee drinker, you know there is nothing more frustrating than looking for coffee and not finding it. Ed decided that since he was usually the first one at school, he would make the coffee.

Now, this sounds simple, and it is, but Ed doesn't drink coffee! He's not making it for himself. He's making it for his people. And when he's standing there in the mail room, ready to pour a cup for one of his teachers and welcome them to another day, he's doing that for culture's sake, not his own.

Ed Morris told me that he has three rules for his teachers. Get your grades in weekly. Take attendance daily. And respond to parent emails. He said that enforcing those policies has gotten a lot smoother since he started making the coffee. His attitude of welcoming others to work, serving them well, and ensuring they have everything they need each day is contagious and has led to his growing influence at that school.

THOUGHTS AND HABITS NOT CONDUCIVE TO LEADERSHIP

I want to close this chapter with a list. If you can't tell by now, I love lists. This list is more of a "what not to do" list than anything else. As leaders, we often think about what we should be doing, but frequently, there's a long list of things that we should stop doing that get ignored.

The list below is adapted from a list published by Rick Rubin in *The Creative Act* (Seriously, get this book.). We leaders must avoid these things, and it is wise to share this with the people we lead. We are all doing the best we can. Letting go of certain habits and attitudes can only make us better leaders of others.

I am going to share this list without elaboration. It stands well on its own.

20 Thoughts and Habits to Avoid as a Leader[51]

1. Believing you're not good enough.
2. Feeling you don't have the energy to lead others.
3. Mistaking rules for truths.
4. Allowing laziness to take over.
5. Settling for less than your best
6. Setting goals so unrealistic you can't even begin to chase them.

7. Thinking you can only lead when the feeling is right.
8. Requiring specific tools or equipment to lead.
9. Abandoning ideas or projects when times get tough.
10. Waiting for permission to start or move ahead.
11. Allowing funding or support needs to get in the way of the work.
12. Spreading yourself too thin to start.
13. Being too busy to finish.
14. Blaming people or circumstances for processes that aren't going well.
15. Allowing negativity to rule.
16. Believing you must be in the mood to lead.
17. Prioritizing other activities over leading your people.
18. Distractibility and procrastination.
19. Impatience.
20. Spending time on things outside of your control.

Becoming a tough and tender leader requires you to choose your attitude well. Great leaders are known as much for what they refuse to do. Consider the list above and ask yourself how many of those behaviors you allow to creep into your daily routine. How can you stop doing them? You are the tone-setter for your organization, classroom, group, or team. Today, decide what habits and thoughts you will set aside to be a tough and tender leader.

THE 1-4-3 – CHAPTER 9: LEADERSHIP – "WHAT COLORS ARE IN YOUR BOX?"

1 Quotable Quote

"Your attitude determines who will join you in your future."

Leadership isn't just about where you're going—it's about who wants to go there with you. Attitude sets the tone for trust, energy, and followership.

4 Key Takeaways

1. **Choose Your Attitude Well:** A choice a leader must make in every situation, every day is: "How do I want to show up today?"
2. **Leadership Is Personal:** Your unique colors, when used well, shape the emotional and cultural tone of your team.
3. **Attitude Is Influence:** How you show up—positively or negatively—colors the way others experience your leadership.
4. **You Don't Need Every Color:** You need to know your own and be willing to share the brush with others.

3 Questions for Your Team

1. What "colors" are most present in your leadership right now? Is anything missing?
2. How would your team describe the emotional tone you bring to the workplace?
3. What's one word you want others to associate with your leadership this year?

10

Excellence – "Environment Not Achievement"

DO YOU REMEMBER the recent AT&T commercials with the theme "Just okay is not okay?" They were hilarious parodies of modern businesses doing a poor job. In one of them, a man goes to a brake shop and asks if they are good at brakes. "We are okay," the worker replies. "Just, okay?" the customer asks. "Yeah, we have a saying here: 'If the brakes don't stop it, something will!'"

As leaders, especially in education, we know that just okay is not okay. No one wants their students to get okay grades. You wouldn't want people to respond "It's okay" when asked about their school. We want them to say, "I LOVE THIS PLACE," of course.

Excellence is the result of a great culture rather than the impetus to it. Culture first, excellence follows. In fact, when coming up with HUSTLE, I was very pleased to put excellence last—not because it's unimportant, but because excellence often happens due to the culture you create as a leader.

Excellence vs. Achievement

We live in an achievement-driven society, where students and teachers are constantly pushed toward checking the box, passing the test, or getting into the best schools. And nowadays, new and better tests are always being developed. Since those tests need to be "coached," new and more expensive coaches, classes, and courses are being introduced to prepare our students.

Some other examples of achievements in schools:

- For Students:
    - GPA
    - Class rank for Valedictorian status
    - SAT and ACT scores
- For Teachers
    - Passing percentage for their AP students.
    - A certain rating on your yearly evaluation.
- For Administrators
    - Graduation rates
    - Performance Indices (my district used the Career and College Readiness Performance Index or CCRPI, an unbreakable imaginary score that made doing your taxes seem like basic math)

- For Coaches
    - o Wins
    - o Championships

While those things are important, great leaders go beyond them. I recently finished a wonderful book by Adam Gopnik called *The Real Work: The Mystery of Mastery.* In it, he uses the work of magicians to discuss excellence. The real work, Gopnik says, "Is the accumulation of skills, craftsmanship, and technical mastery that can only be achieved by years of consistent commitment."[52] He challenges the us to "stop chasing evanescent achievements and move toward enduring accomplishments."[53]

When we drive our people toward achievements, we often forget that what motivates us is the thrill of accomplishment. Mastering something profoundly difficult, usually with others, is the real work. Stepping up to challenges and overcoming obstacles, rather than being overwhelmed by them, is the hallmark of the feeling of success that drives us to keep coming back repeatedly. It's the journey, not the destination.

It can also be argued that many of the most impactful and memorable moments we experienced in school didn't happen in the classroom or during the school day. They were likely on a field, in a gym, in our fine arts rooms, in a cafeteria, on a trip, in a locker room, etc.

What is required of our leaders to get our schools to prioritize accomplishments over achievements is the idea of **consistent commitment.**

TAKING THE LEAD

Several years ago, my wife, Aaren, and I took up rock climbing. There's a local gym near our house where we can climb indoors. It's a great workout and something that we can do together. Rock climbing is an interesting sport because it requires you to be strong, smart, and to conquer your fears. Getting to the top of a sixty-foot wall, letting go so your belayer (the person responsible for your safety) can lower you, is still unsettling after many years.

After we had been climbing for a while, Aaren and I wanted to climb outdoors. There are some great spots about two hours from our house. To climb outdoors, we needed a different set of skills. We had to learn how to lead-climb, set an anchor, clean the anchor, and then rappel down. There's a lot to it!

When you're lead climbing, the rope hangs down toward your feet, and as you go, you have to pause, reach down, grab it, and clip it into "quickdraws" (carabiners) that you have placed in bolts on the wall. The draws are six to eight feet apart, meaning falling off the wall meant dropping six to eight feet before the rope caught you. It can be terrifying. More than once, I've wanted to quit during a climb, because I was tired or scared. Two things kept me going: encouragement from my wife on the ground, keeping me safe, and cheering me on, and the fact that my mission when I started the climb was to reach the top.

To call yourself a rock climber, your mission must be to reach the top. When the going gets tough, when the call to descend to comfort and safety is strong, the committed keep going. Great leaders model commitment in their team by consistently showing up, day in and day out.

Those leaders are there in the good times and the bad. They're consistent through challenges and committed to the mission. When it comes to tough and tender leadership, commitment comes with the territory.

There are two truths about commitment that I want us to remember:

1. Commitment is a decision to act.
2. Consistency is staying resilient with that action when things get hard.

Making decisions is what leaders do. It's been said that the average person makes about 10,000 decisions a day. I believe that leaders make many more. And the best leaders, who drive I LOVE THIS PLACE culture, stay true to their choices when the going gets tough. Of course, that doesn't mean you stick to the course when the course is clearly wrong. But it means you stick by your word, show up daily, and maintain your leadership values.

MODELING COMMITMENT TO THOSE YOU LEAD

I want to get practical here. The best way to get people to commit is to show your level of commitment to them. It stands to reason that you, the leader, would be the most committed. Remember, "The speed of the leader is the speed of the team." Let's work on our commitment as a benchmark for our team.

Make Certain Decisions Only Once

Reducing your mental load is a key to keeping your commitments. Often, our "misses" are not because we don't care but because we forgot (or had too many things going on… dropping plates). You aren't wearied by an additional decision when you pre-decide certain things.

One example of this from my leadership journey had to do with fundraising. Later in my career, I decided that we were not going to sell things to raise funds anymore. I wanted to focus on hosting events and crowdfunding initiatives. Suppose you've been in educational leadership for more than one day. In that case, you know the number of contact requests you get from companies wanting to sell cheesecake, wrapping paper, cookies, bedsheets, etc. I would tell my high schoolers to get out early b/c once the Girl Scouts start up, they'll lose every time. You cannot outsell a cute kid armed with thin mint cookies.

Having decided that we wouldn't sell, it became easy to say no to those people. I could say, "No thanks, we don't do those fundraisers." Plus, I had people who could act as gatekeepers for me. They could "pre-deny" those requests because they knew we had already decided not to do them. Making decisions once is a great way to clear your plate for the bigger decisions that require your attention.

Use Commitment Devices

Commitment devices are a crucial part of a leader's day. Examples of commitment devices are alarms, reminders, and people. These external forces remind you or hold you accountable for your decisions. It's like a trick you play on your future self to keep you committed.

I'm a part of a men's group called F3 that works out at 5:30 a.m. six days a week. While that may seem ridiculously early, as a dad and a husband, my free time is early morning before everyone gets up. I don't exercise after work. That's my time with my wife and kids.

To make sure I stay committed to these workouts, I use alarms, reminders, and people. First, I set an alarm on my watch. It vibrates, so it only wakes me up, not my wife (You can't work out if you're dead, and that's what I'd be if I woke Aaren at 5 a.m.).

Second, the reminder. The night before, I place my workout clothes and shoes on the floor beside my bed. When I wake up and see them, it's my "yesterday self" reminding my "today self" about the commitment that I'd made to exercise.

Finally, people. Our group uses the app Slack to keep everyone up to date with plans for workouts and events, and Slack allows for custom emojis as responses. One of our emojis is "HC." It stands for "hard commit." If you tap the HC emoji for a workout, you'd better show up. Backing out on an HC will undoubtedly lead to endless ribbing and callouts from your friends and workout buddies. It keeps me honest. It's a commitment device I use the night before to trick myself into getting up and moving when the 5 a.m. alarm goes off.

Often, a commitment device is as simple as telling someone your plans. If you inform a teacher you will visit or observe their class, you are more likely to show up. Not showing up in that case will result in a loss of influence. Committed leaders move mountains to keep influence with those they lead.

Coaching Yourself

This is my favorite way to approach committing to decisions. You likely know that coaching strategies involve asking a lot of questions. Coaching isn't about giving advice; it's about asking the right questions to get the person you're coaching to use what they already know to solve an issue. As leaders, we face innumerable problems, puzzles, and perplexing decisions every day. And often, we don't have a coach to help us.

In this case, there is one key question to ask yourself: **"What Would a Great ________ Do?"** The answer will likely become obvious when you ask yourself this question and fill in the blank.

Let's say you need to visit a teacher's classroom, but you have parent emails to answer. Ask yourself, "What would a great leader do?" You're likely going to respond, "Visit the teacher." The emails will still be there when you get back.

When you ask, "What would a great leader do?" you're no longer faced with a choice of what action to take. Instead, you're faced with the choice between being a **great** leader or a **mediocre** one. That's an easier decision because you wouldn't have gotten this far into a leadership book if you wanted to be mediocre.

This applies to parents and spouses as well. When my wife is folding the laundry and I'm watching TV, I often ask myself, "What would a great husband do?" The answer is clear: He would help his wife. At that moment, my internal conversation shifts to whether I want to be a **mediocre** or a **great** husband. I can't say I always choose to be great, but at least I'm being honest with myself!

Here's another way to think about it. Suppose you aren't sure what to do. Choose the option that is most inconvenient for you at the time. If the decision were easy, people would make it more often. It's inconvenient for me to get off the couch and help. Answering emails is more convenient than visiting classrooms.

Did you know that mediocre is a rock-climbing term? Mediocre comes from two Latin words meaning "middle (medius) of the rock (ocris)." A mediocre rock climber stops in the middle of the rock and goes back down. Perhaps the climb got too hard. Maybe the climber had another appointment, and the climb took too long. Perhaps they forgot why they started and just gave up. Mediocre leaders lose their commitment to the mission for those same reasons.

Keep your commitments. You'll begin to see the same in others, and in doing so, you are creating an environment where excellence can happen every day. Because, as you're about to see, excellence is not that hard to find.

THE TURK AND A CULTURE OF EXCELLENCE[54]

In 1770, Wolfgang von Kempelen, an Austrian inventor and showman, debuted the Mechanical Turk. The Turk, as they called it, was an automated chess-playing machine. The machine itself was a wooden cabinet that housed a life-sized figure of a Turk dressed in Ottoman robes and a turban. The Turk was sitting behind a chessboard.

The Turk delighted and captivated audiences across the globe as it seemingly played chess against live opponents. Not only did it play, but it also played well! The Turk defeated many famous opponents, including Benjamin Franklin and Napoleon, as well as many chess masters across the globe. In addition, the Turk could communicate with audiences via letterboard and even correct mistakes (purposeful and otherwise) of its opponents who tried vainly to trick the machine.

By all accounts, Kempelen had somehow created the world's first artificial intelligence. People believed this for eighty-four years until 1854 when a fire destroyed the museum where it was being kept. After that, Kempelen's son published the Turk's secret.

Surprise! The Turk was a hoax—a brilliant hoax, but a hoax nonetheless. Inside the cabinet beneath the Turk figure, there was just enough room for a chess player to fit and operate the machine. Through an intricate series of magnets and levers, an actual human played chess against opponents.

Of course, you must be wondering how Kempelen convinced master chess players to get inside a box and play as if they were machines. Here's the thing: he didn't! Kempelen would go to a city and sneak into the local chess club. He would find good (not great) chess players and offer to pay them to get inside the box and play as the Turk. The fascinating part about this story is that the good chess players became great chess players when they got into the box.

You see, excellence never takes place outside of the context of performance. There wasn't any magic to the improvement of the chess players while they were in the box; the **environment** made them great. While they couldn't be seen, they knew playing as the Turk was a big deal. It was bigger than them, and they rose to the challenge.

That is precisely what great culture does for the people you lead. Excellence becomes greater because of the context in which it is expected. When you show that you are committed to the mission and the people on your team, excellence will take care of itself. That's why it's last on the list.

Becoming a humble, understanding, scholarly, and trustworthy leader with a great attitude who is committed to excellence creates an environment for people to thrive. It starts with you putting your Turk box together and convincing people to get inside. Within that environment, people will produce results that are much greater than achievements that fade with time.

Let the culture of your organization be your greatest enduring accomplishment.

And if you're not sure your people are up for it, remember this: Kempelen didn't need chess masters in the box. He needed willing, good players. Of course, that begs the question, why not get masters? First off, masters were hard to find, and likely harder to convince. They were also not necessary. Kempelen knew something that every great leader must learn:

Excellence isn't uncommon. It's everywhere.
It just needs the right environment.

Of course, you want to hire and empower the best possible people. But what if you must settle for a good teacher instead of a great one? What if the choice for a football coach is a good coach but not a superstar with an impeccable record? What, then, should we do? Remember the Turk.

Inside the box was someone good who was put into an environment that made their performance great. That's the importance of culture. I like to imagine the young chess player sitting inside that box, doing work that no one can see, just in awe of what they could accomplish.

That same feeling can exist at your place. You need to create the right environment for people to perform. When you do, you will begin to experience the amplification of your culture. When we grow more leaders, the real magic starts to happen.

THE 1-4-3 – CHAPTER 10: EXCELLENCE – "ENVIRONMENT NOT ACHIEVEMENT"

1 Quotable Quote

"Excellence isn't uncommon. It's everywhere. It just needs the right environment."

If you want to raise the bar, don't just push harder—build better. Culture creates excellence long before achievement proves it.

4 Key Takeaways

1. **Leaders set the standard**: What you expect, repeat, and model becomes the norm for everyone else.
2. **Environments shape people:** If your culture expects excellence, you'll get more of it. If it tolerates mediocrity, you'll get that.
3. **Excellence isn't rare—it's often just untapped:** People have greatness in them, but the right environment draws it out.
4. **Accountability and encouragement are both culture builders:** Culture gets stronger when leaders call people *up*, not just *out*. You need both belief and boundaries if you want people to grow.

3 Questions for Your Team

1. What messages does your environment send about what's expected and what's accepted?
2. Where in your school or team are you seeing excellence? Why?
3. What's one part of your school environment that could better support excellence?

11

Amplify Your Culture

I SPENT SEVENTEEN years teaching music to students. But you may be wondering, why did you leave the classroom? Did I face the same burnout and bad culture that I've been railing against this entire book? The answer is no. I never had a bad principal. I taught in a great community. Not a day goes by that I don't miss my students.

There came a time, however, when I realized that I enjoyed teaching leadership and building culture more than I enjoyed teaching music. It was during the 2020 COVID-19 pandemic that I realized I was ready to do something more with my passion. At first, I thought I wanted to be a school principal. As luck would have it, there were no jobs available at that time for me to pursue. When Growing Leaders posted a job for a curriculum director, I realized my time had come. I had the opportunity to take the amazing culture of leadership we had built and share that with the world through my work.

I started the book with two big ideas. First, **by growing as a leader, I can add value to my school and community.**

My goal so far has been to show you the power of your leadership and how it affects culture. I gave you a framework for becoming a tough and tender leader and showed you that "Good things come to leaders who HUSTLE."

The premise of this book, however, started with a quote from a teacher who felt unsupported and unseen in their community. It read:

> *"Teachers need positive and productive support. We try to give as much as we can (financially, emotionally, physically, mentally) to help our students succeed—and sometimes—even that is not enough. The school used to be the 'heart' of the community."*[55]

It's on to big idea number two:

I can amplify that value by growing <u>others</u> as leaders.

My goal with these final chapters is to show how leadership affects culture and is the secret to recruiting new teachers, retaining your best teachers, and reclaiming your school's place at the heart of the community. Multiplied value is what's needed. None of us are big enough to do this job alone. It requires others. And it may not surprise you that I want to introduce this concept with a music metaphor—resonance.

RESONANCE

The term resonance refers to a deep, reverberating fullness of sound. It's the voice that you use when pretending to be a radio host. It's the sound that you hear when a well-tuned engine starts up. In music, resonance is the quality and quantity of the sound that the musician makes with their instrument and how those sounds relate to one another.

I spent a lot of time teaching resonance, both to individuals and groups. Quality of sound is a topic we discuss every day. As you'll see below, resonance is always important. The challenge of teaching music is that every student's individual contribution matters, but they must also consider how they mesh with their peers.

If I'm playing all the right notes at the correct volume, but my quality of sound doesn't match everyone else's, I'm going to stick out like a sore thumb. I will make the group sound bad. If I choose to play too soft and no one hears it, then the group is not maximizing its potential. The combination of volume, frequency, and quality of sound is essential to every musical performance. Let's go a bit deeper.

Sound travels in waves that resemble sine waves in math. They have peaks and valleys. The height of the peaks is the volume of the sound (how loud), and the distance between them is the frequency of the sound (how high or low in pitch). When two musicians make a sound at the same time, the waves achieve what is called **superposition**.

Superposition is how acousticians talk about waves that interact when passing through the same medium (like the air in the room on the way to your ears). When sound waves interact, they create what is called interference (I know it's all science-y… but it's about to get GOOOOOD).

There are two types of interference: destructive and constructive.

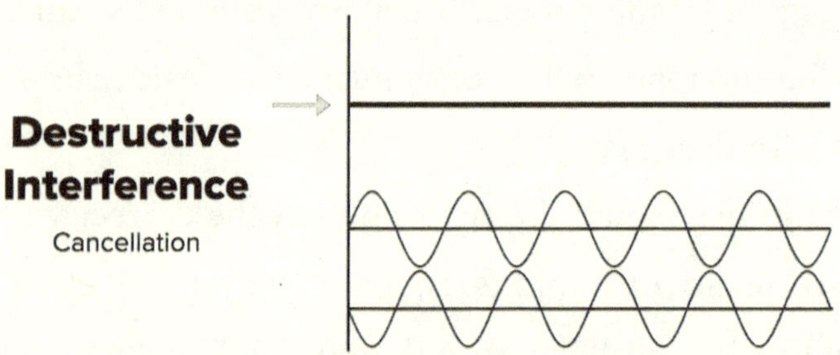

Destructive interference occurs when two waves collide, and their peaks and valleys are opposite one another. The result is the cancellation of sound. This is the principle that noise-cancelling headphones use. Your headphones create a sound that is the opposite of the sounds around you. It cancels out the room noise.

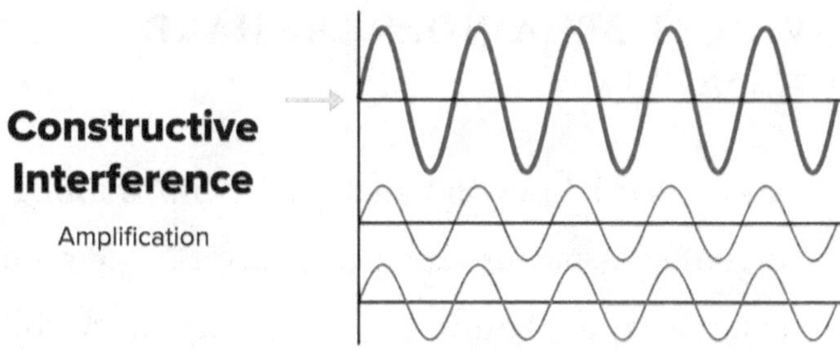

Constructive interference (which sounds like an oxymoron, I know… thanks, science) is the opposite. When two waves collide whose peaks and valleys match, the result is amplification. The sound created is louder and more resonant than before. Getting musicians to play "in tune" is the art of having them create sound waves that match, thus resulting in better, more resonant, and amplified sounds.

The secret is getting your musicians on the same wavelength—the same frequency. You see it now, don't you? Leadership training works the same way. Growing your leaders and empowering them in the vision and mission of your school gets people on the same frequency.

Leadership development is how you amplify your culture. Doing so sends out waves that help recruit better people, retain your best people, and reclaim your school's place at the heart of the community!

INDIVIDUAL BEHAVIORS ARE HARD TO CHANGE

It may be hard to accept that leadership training can change ingrained behaviors and perspectives in your school, but it can. Suzanne Smith at Social Impact Architects describes a "social ripple effect" of how change works in communities. Their research has found that individual behaviors are very hard to change. However, individual behaviors are overwhelmingly affected by environments.

The social ripple effect tells us that if we can co-create environments that support individual change, then individuals can act in small groups to create a chain reaction that stimulates cultural change.[56] That chain reaction of ripples acts like the sound waves we just talked about amplifying.

If we intentionally grow leaders, they can work together to impact their circles and teams. Your school is likely already set up with teams to do this! Schools have clubs, classes, sports, curriculum teams, grade levels, professional learning communities, departments, etc. A school environment is set up for success; it's just a matter of leveraging the teams to make it happen.

As you create more teams that impact one another, the school begins to be affected. Your academic classes become stronger and more connected as teachers become more connected leaders. The arts and athletic groups grow because they have better coaches.

Once the school culture has changed, the community will start to notice, and you'll begin to attract new hires and students, retain your best hires and students, and your stakeholders will start to give back.

I Love This Place culture ripples out like amplified sound waves to homes, banks, churches, businesses, and even ballot boxes. And the beauty of sending waves out is when they come back. One example of how this worked in my organization came from Nathan Jones and his idea to "march out hunger" in our community.

Marching Out Hunger

Nathan Jones moved into our district as a freshman. This "preacher's kid" didn't know anyone because he didn't attend our local middle schools. Nathan did know that our community's needs were not being met. His dad pastored a local church, and they saw needs that the rest of us did not.

Nathan came to me early on with a question and an idea. He wanted to know if I knew how many kids in our surrounding areas didn't get to eat when they weren't at school. I didn't know. He also wanted us to use our organizational influence to make a difference for those kids.

It was not my finest leadership moment, but I told Nathan to let me think about it, and we would chat later. I saw a ninth grader standing in front of me, whom I barely knew, trying to create more work for all of us. I missed the point.

Our "chat later" came after two years. At this point, Nathan had become an influential leader in our program. He had just become our "band president" elected by his peers. He saw his moment and returned to me with his idea of "Marching Out Hunger."

Nathan came in with a plan, a partner organization, and a group of students on his team to help. This time, he was not seeking my help, just my permission. Nathan had been a part of our leadership development program for two years. His favorite lesson was one we called the Starving Baker (I have to feed myself before I can feed others). He knew that people needed to be fed to be fruitful, and he was ready to make that happen.

His plan was for us to run a fundraising drive for October, our busiest month. Students would be challenged to raise $100 a piece. That money would go toward the supplies to pack meals, which we would then deliver to local elementary schools the week before Thanksgiving break. On breaks like these, many students go hungry because they don't have access to school breakfast and lunch.

That year, we raised $5,000 to feed children in our community. Students assembled in teams and packed 2,000 meals to deliver to local schools.

The next year, Nathan wanted to raise the bar. We added a "lock-in" to the fundraising goal. (Kids don't want to go to school in the morning but love to be locked into school all night… makes sense.) After we packed the meals together, any student who raised $100 got to spend an entire night in the school with their teachers and friends, playing games, watching movies, and eating pizza. We raised over $10,000 in three weeks!

We also took students to the local elementary schools. It was Nathan's idea to have lunch with the students at their school and then give them meal bags on their way back to class. You would have thought we brought celebrities to those schools. The connection and impact were truly amazing to see. And it was student-leader-driven, not by me, but by those I had equipped and empowered.

A local newspaper came by and interviewed Nathan during the event, and he said this:

> People are so focused on social media that they forget the people around them. We want to encourage

> everyone to find love from the people around them, not the likes from those who are far away.[57]

Wise words from a seventeen-year-old. The year after Nathan graduated, we raised $22,000 in two weeks. This food went to our community, Haiti, and Ukraine, extending our impact globally. He started an incredible Ripple Effect that impacted the entire world. Nathan helped us to create an I LOVE THIS PLACE culture. And I want to help you create it in your place. In the next chapter, I want to lay out the specific steps we took to grow leaders in our organization on a regular basis.

THE 1-4-3 – CHAPTER 11: AMPLIFY YOUR CULTURE

1 Quotable Quote

"Leadership development is how you amplify your culture."

You can't do it all, but you can scale your impact by growing others to live out the values, attitudes, and expected behaviors that make up a great school.

4 Key Takeaways

1. **Amplify, Don't Just Add:** Leadership impact grows when you build leaders, not just when you do more.
2. **Create Leadership Opportunities:** Culture shifts when people are empowered and trusted to lead in real ways.
3. **Replace Fear with Responsibility:** Growth happens when people are free to take risks and own results.
4. **Leadership Is About People:** Don't focus on fixing problems—focus on developing people.

3 Questions for Your Team

1. How are you actively growing leaders?
2. Where might you be limiting growth by doing too much yourself?
4. What small leadership opportunity could you give someone this week?

12

"I Love This Place" in Your Place

THE MOST STRESSFUL days of the year for a band director are registration days, when new members are deciding if they will join your program, and current members are deciding if they want to stay. There are many factors at play with the schedule of a high school student, of course. They are weighing future plans, other electives, sports involvement, dual enrollment, job opportunities, scholarships, etc. Even knowing all these things, I still struggled not to take it personally when a student elected not to stay in band class or not join as a freshman. It just felt like they were choosing someone else over me. Of course, that's ridiculous, but if you've ever coached anything, I think you understand what I mean.

I always wished I could control their decisions, somehow thinking I knew better. Most leaders struggle with control. Realizing what you can control, what you cannot, and where you have influence can be life-changing for a leader. Here's a helpful reminder:

I control my leadership.

I can become a tough and tender leader for the people around me.

I cannot control the community or the people I lead.

This includes what they think of our school. Don't waste energy trying.

I can influence and grow the leaders in my building.

With my guidance, I can give others ownership to use their influence to change the culture inside and outside the building.

As you become a better leader, use what you've learned to guide others into being better leaders. Because you are guiding them using principles you are already practicing, you are getting your people on the same wavelength. And we know what happens then: **amplification**.

Growing more leaders in our schools is the key to re-capturing the heart of the community. Infusing connection and high standards by being tough and tender and intentionally teaching others how to do the same is a great place to start.

LEADERSHIP TRAINING IS PREDICTIVE OF BEHAVIOR

There are additional and wonderful by-products to intentional leadership training in schools. When people feel seen, loved, and challenged, predicting how they will respond to certain situations is easier. BambooHR's research has found that the impact of culture that stems from great leadership leads to:

- Higher Engagement
- More Creativity and Innovation
- Increased Empathy and Belonging
- Improved Morale
- Greater Ability to Attract Top Talent
- Higher Retention[58]

These are wonderful things we would all want to happen! This begs the question, why don't we train leaders more often? I think a lack of leadership training rarely stems from a lack of effort or desire to grow leaders. **Instead, it stems from a lack of good tools and an implementation strategy.** Given the right tools and strategy, any and every school can invest in its leaders in a real, tangible way.

In 2016, I met Dr. Tim Elmore and learned about his leadership curriculum, which we now call iLead. I had been searching for ways to engage all my students and staff in leadership training, and this was the solution we needed.

Our leadership development program for the next six years looked like this:

- On Wednesdays in the first semester, we took time out of regular instruction for all classes to learn leadership together. We reached an average of 300 students daily (about 15 percent of the entire school).
- Initially, we focused on self-leadership, using many of the themes you've encountered in the chapters thus far. Sometimes, the lessons took the entire class, other times, less. The time spent varied based on our conversations.
- In the second semester, we moved leadership training to after school. We had performance evaluations in March and couldn't spare the full day of instruction then. We averaged over 100 students volunteering to participate in this fifteen-week after-school program.

We impacted many students with leadership training, and the results were incredible. To quantify the results, I will use every music program's most valuable metrics: recruiting and retention (Actually, all electives and sports live and die on these two—it's tough to coach empty chairs.).

The reason why recruiting and retention were so important to us lies in the nature of most high school music programs. We didn't have end-of-course tests or state-mandated individual assessments. Our grades didn't even count on most scholarship transcripts. Career-wise, we sent around 1 percent of our students to college to study to become professional musicians or music teachers. Our students joined and stayed in our classes for reasons other than GPA or career choice. It was because they benefited from the musical and leadership instruction that carried a value greater than a grade or a job.

Looking at ten years' worth of enrollment data, I came to some conclusions about the effects of leadership training on the people I was leading. Adding leadership development was nearly the only thing that changed during these ten years. I was the leader the entire time, and the core of our staff stayed the same. The only major change (albeit huge) was the pandemic that took us out of our "normal" in 2020.

In the data, I looked for two main items:

1. **What percentage of students stayed in the program for four years (ninth to twelfth grade)?** These students were our highly committed students who sacrificed other things to stay in music.

2. **What did our recruiting numbers look like?** Sustaining our numbers depended on convincing eighth-grade students to join. What was our reputation in the community?

Retention Data

Before the leadership implementation, 52 percent of our students would stay for all four years. This is not bad at all. After we started leadership development, this increased to 59 percent! That's an average of twenty-one more students per year. And as I looked deeper, I discovered something very interesting.

I looked at the likelihood that students would stay from their second year through graduation. Pre-leadership, if students stayed in the band into tenth grade, they were 77 percent likely to remain until graduation. With leadership development, that statistic rose to 82 percent. Getting students from ninth to tenth grade is key. Looking at that data, students were 7 percent more likely to stay with us from ninth to tenth grade due to the influence of leadership development in their lives.

How interesting! Those were our youngest students, and leadership training empowered them to stay with us for the long haul.

Remember, back to the beginning of the book, the research into Millennial and Gen X teachers says that they value culture and leadership more than (or at least as much as) salary and benefits. Those teachers will likely stay and grow with us if we get them plugged into intentional leadership training early.

One important note: our leadership program involved our youngest people engaging directly with me, their leader, and older students who had been with us for a while. Leadership training for young staff that involves a direct connection with their leaders and older mentor teachers is a great way to influence the culture of your school. We just needed a tool that helped us to make it happen.

Recruiting Data

The other big data piece that needed to be examined was recruiting. When people leave (or graduate), how good are we at replacing them? We can't train our youngest leaders if none exist!

I mentioned earlier that the year before we started leadership development with our students, we saw an incredible drop in recruiting success. One year, we had 121 incoming students, and the next, it dropped to eighty-two. Big problem! For some reason, our reputation in the community had taken a hit.

Adding leadership training and empowering our young leaders to impact the community made a big difference. Before our efforts, our recruiting growth rate was around 9 percent. It was very consistent. Then, we took a big hit. After implementing this program, our recruiting growth skyrocketed to 69.5 percent! That eighty-two-student incoming class in 2016 grew to an incoming class of 139 students in 2022. This was the largest we had ever seen. Growing leaders made a huge difference.

Two things that made this possible. First, I became a better leader. I needed to grow and learn about leadership myself. Second, we increased the number of leaders who were willing and able to impact the community and spread our reputation far and wide. Our leaders' willingness to go out and say, "I Love this Place, and you will too," was a major difference in the growth of our program.

Your people are your best recruiters. Leadership training and culture building can be the secret to attracting top talent to apply for openings at your school.

PUTTING LEADERSHIP TRAINING INTO PRACTICE

I have shared with you a plan that worked for my organization. I'm not here to tell you exactly how to do this; I want to encourage you to try it. As we all know, leadership training can have a major impact on people; we sometimes lack either the intentionality or the tools (or both) to put it into practice.

There are three things that every leader should consider when getting their leadership training plan off the ground:

1. How are you going to make time for the training?
2. What tools are you going to use for the training?
3. Who is going to be involved in the training?

Make Time for Training

This can be the biggest challenge for any school. There's no time! I mentioned earlier that I had to be courageous enough to pause instruction to make time for leadership training. Look at what I just said—I had to be **courageous** enough to **make time** for leadership training.

I would be lying if I said everyone was excited about my leadership training plan. Not every student wanted leadership training, and not every staff member thought the students needed it. In fact, my staff initially declined to participate in the training because they either disagreed that it was necessary or didn't think they had the skills to lead it.

As the organization's leader, I had to prioritize making this happen. While it took some convincing, the results speak for themselves. A school leader could implement leadership training in several ways. Lunch and Learn, PLC meetings, staff meetings, after-school leadership cohorts, and monthly professional development all come to mind.

The important aspect here is that you make it a priority and stay courageous in the process for the training to take hold. I encourage you, leader, to facilitate the training. This way, your people can see your heart for leadership and understand how your vision will impact them and the school. You may have to find creative ways to give them time back or, at the very least, provide some food. Teachers will come to a meeting that has food.

Find Tools That Create Waves Instead of Splashes

Throughout my career, I tried various strategies for leadership training. It started with bringing in people to facilitate the training. We would have a big kickoff event with all our leaders, get all excited about the potential, and then set off to change the world. The problem with those big "splashy" leader events is that the effects rarely last as long as you need them to. It can be a great way to start, but you need a tool that can create waves. (Yes, another metaphor.)

One of our iLead lessons uses the metaphor of *Splashes and Waves*. It's a reminder that making a splash is relatively easy compared to making waves. You've been to the beach,

I'm sure. No amount of splashing around will compare to the power of one of those big, powerful waves in the ocean. The same goes for leadership training. Regular meetings with an effective tool are the best way to drive change. Waves take time. But waves are powerful.

I have mentioned this a few times, but the best tool I have found for developing leaders is iLead. iLead lessons start with memorable images, lead to meaningful conversations, and end with people making better choices and making changes to grow. The power of leadership lessons in this format is both the image as an anchor and the connection power of discussion.

The best part about iLead is that it's set up in an easy-to-use sequence. The lessons are fully fleshed out for anyone to facilitate, and each lesson comes with easy-to-share follow-up. We use this concept from kindergarten to adulthood. I'm talking leadership development from recess to retirement! If I haven't convinced you yet, I won't. The message is to find a useful tool and implement it regularly and intentionally. Change happens in waves, not splashes.

Who Are You Training?

The last step is to determine who gets the training. Not everyone may need it, or you may be ready to train only your leadership team and then empower them to train others. There are several different ways to determine who to include.

My method was to give everyone a taste and then to draw in those who wanted more. In giving everyone a taste, I learned two things. First, I realized who was hungry to lead. I could tell this by how they engaged. Second, I determined who was willing to pay a higher price to lead. This was important because the meetings that followed were after school and not always convenient. I didn't offer those to everyone. Only those willing to give something up can make it happen.

Everyone deserves to be led well. Everyone deserves to learn how to lead well. There are stages, though. In determining who your high-impact leaders are, consider the following criteria:

1. Who do others look to in the building? Who has influence?
2. Who might bring new ideas to the table that are different than yours?
3. Who is willing to pay the price to lead?
4. Who is the next generation of leaders that will carry the torch when you're gone?

As I wrote those questions, I was reminded of two student leaders I had the privilege of working with for several years, Logan and Layth. Logan and Layth had larger-than-life personalities, and as a result, they had a certain level of influence. Logan could be heard from 100 yards away with a booming "HELLOOOOO" to anyone and everyone. Layth went as far as becoming our mascot, "Harry the Hawk," to be able to use his personality to entertain people.

I'm not sure I've ever seen two young men impact a school quite like they did. But without leadership training and mentorship, it could have all been wasted energy.

As I watched them grow, I knew they were special, but were they willing to pay the price to lead and grow up the next generation to lead behind them? The answer was a resounding yes. Logan would take his French Horn on vacation with him. He would come back from breaks and entertain us with story upon story about where he practiced his French Horn and how he was able to entertain complete strangers with his music. Logan's willingness to hold himself accountable and to share about it made practicing "cool" for other students. You can't imagine how hard that is to do!

Layth was everyone's friend, connecting with wildly different groups of people. In four years, I'm not sure he missed a day of school or rehearsal. He was willing to pay the price. Layth mentored countless students younger than him, making sure they knew the importance of showing up, giving their full effort, and, above all, being authentic to others.

Logan and Layth were key members of a core group of leaders who made our culture great. All they needed was some instruction and tools to set them on the right path and the opportunity to lead. I helped them find both and then freed them to lead others. They were both tough and tender leaders to their peers.

Creating and developing a team of leaders with influence, new ideas, a hunger to lead, and the energy to impact others is a dangerous combination. As Mister Rogers said, "Look for the helpers." Great leaders find those willing to embrace toughness, tenderness, and hustle. Then they empower them to amplify impact.

THE 1-4-3 – CHAPTER 12: "I LOVE THIS PLACE" IN YOUR PLACE

1 Quotable Quote

"Growing more leaders in our schools is the key to re-capturing the heart of the community."

You can't overhaul the world, but you can ignite the leaders in front of you. That's how "I love this place" moves from a mere phrase to a transformational reality.

4 Key Takeaways

1. Culture begins with you—but it can't end with you: Great leadership doesn't stop at personal growth. It amplifies and multiplies.
2. Model First, Then Multiply: Leadership becomes contagious when others see it consistently lived out.
3. Amplify by Empowering: Guiding others to lead creates a multiplying effect on school culture.
4. Culture Spread: "I love this place" isn't limited to one room—it can ripple through buildings, teams, and communities.

3 Questions for Your Team

1. Who in your building or circle needs to be invited into leadership—and what may be holding them back?
2. How can you move from leading alone to leading alongside others?
3. How can you intentionally spread the culture you want through the school and into your community?

13

It's Not About Us

I HAVE WAITED this entire book to introduce you to Brenna. She stands as one of the greatest young leaders I have ever met. I taught Brenna's older sister, so I had known her and her family for years. Brenna plays the Oboe like a professional. What a dream to teach such a mature musician. However, as angelic as her sound is, the person making the sounds may be more so.

Brenna came to me with an idea to solve a problem she saw in her school. In her eyes, the special needs population was not given enough opportunities. She discovered an organization called United Sound that empowered young leaders with resources and opportunities to mentor students with special needs to learn music.

Brenna came to me with a plan, supporters, and a vision. Just like Nathan, she didn't need my help; she needed my permission and support. Brenna contacted United Sound and set up a meeting to get started. She contacted our special education teachers and got permission to visit their classes.

She had recruited her peers to help her as mentors. She was ready.

The rest was truly magical. Every Friday, at 3:30 p.m., our new musicians would come to the band room to meet with their peer mentors. Working in groups of three, the band students would help the new musicians learn to hold the instruments, make basic sounds on them, and walk them through some adaptive music notation to learn to make sounds at the right time. They would also play games to get to know one another. To top it all off, each new musician was presented with a certificate welcoming them as a "member of the band." They cultivated true belonging.

I was there as a supervisor but did not teach or lead. My job was to take pictures and, in awe, watch young people mentoring other young people. They had even contacted the new musicians' parents to arrange pick-up times and walked them to their cars when they were finished!

Brenna's vision didn't stop with after-school practices. She wanted them to play with us at our year's final concert. Having chosen the music for the new musicians' performance, she instructed them to wear their fanciest prom attire and arranged for them to visit our class to rehearse with the band. Brenna even asked if she could conduct the performance, to which I happily obliged.

The result was life-changing for everyone involved and culture-defining.

Our final concert was at a large local amphitheater, with thousands in attendance. The United Sound performance was placed last in the program. When we got to that point, Brenna took the microphone and introduced them individually as they approached the stage in sequined gowns and tuxedos. They stood out big time because the rest of the band wore all black, which was all by design.

As the band played "You've Got a Friend In Me" together, the mentors stood over their new musician friends, helping them make sounds at the right time. There were wrong notes and entrances, weird honks and squawks, but the whole thing ended with a standing ovation and misty eyes all over the house.

If you want to see it for yourself, I made a video – https://tinyurl.com/HillgroveUnitedSound.

(I'm not crying, you're crying.)

The impact of United Sound on the band was obvious. It was the impact it had on our school culture that perhaps I didn't expect. The following year, we saw major increases in inclusion on our campus. Students began the "Friends Club," a student-led club for students with special needs to hang out with peers from all parts of the school. Our cheer squad started "Crimson Pride," a special needs cheerleading program. We even saw our students with special needs celebrated at pep rallies, the entire school cheering and encouraging a group of students who are often overlooked.

The amplification effect of Brenna's idea and my decision to let her chase it went well beyond what any of us expected. In all the beautiful stories I've told in these final chapters, we see two things in common:

First, we see leaders making an enormous impact on their school, which rippled into the community to create change. There was a sizable uptick in money donated to our organization as a direct result of the reputation we created together. The year after I left, they raised over $40,000 in a month to serve the students' needs. That's evidence of ripples going out and coming right back.

The other thing these stories have in common is something we often miss. I dismissed Nathan initially because I thought his idea meant more work for me, the leader. I was hesitant to empower Logan and Layth because of what might happen if they failed. I was initially frustrated with Brenna over what seemed like another program to manage. What I neglected to see at first was that they weren't looking for me to do anything. **They were looking for the freedom to practice the leadership I had taught them.**

When we lead with humility, understanding, scholarship, trust, leadership habits and attitudes, and high standards of excellence, we can free others up to lead. When we equip others with skills and empower them with our permission and trust, we can create more ripples that impact school and community culture. Simply put:

Amplification Happens When People Know They Are Free to Lead.

Give people the skills and the permission to make things happen, and you will not regret the results.

LONG AFTER WE ARE GONE

Just like highly resonant sound waves reverberate long after the sound source has stopped, the culture you help create can be around long after you're gone. We might not even be there to see the best days of the school. If we do this right, people will continue to say, "I Love This Place," but they might forget who started the movement in the first place. When we grow leaders and empower them with the freedom to lead, we begin a ripple effect that will continue long after our presence is needed.

About a year after I left to take this new job, I was reminded that the ripples were still moving without me there. My wife got a text message from a friend that looked like this:

GM I'm reminded that your hubby is a pretty popular guy when his name comes up in my sales meeting with an interior designer this morning

Stop!! That's hysterical

Right?! I met the designer for the 1st time...her daughter is graduating this year from H'Grove, BUT her son is coming up from Lovinggood to be in Marching Band.....cuz of your hubby & the program reputation.

That's quite a lasting ripple effect...so awesome

Quite a lasting ripple effect indeed. I don't take credit for this change. The intentional growth and leadership training of the people around me made it happen. It wasn't about me, it was about impact. It was about creating lasting ripples that will continue after we leave the place we are leading, even more so when we give rocks to others to create their own ripples.

Remember, you alone cannot change your community or your culture, but you can cast many stones to create ripples that can.

BOLAND'S BUDDIES

I'm often asked if there is a leader that I believe embodies the ideals of tough and tender leadership. Leaders I speak to want to know if this is just theory, or if someone has applied these principles to great success as a school leader. Meet my first principal, Mr. Joseph Boland. In 2006, Mr. Boland was tasked with opening our brand-new high school. Having been a well-respected teacher, coach, assistant principal, and principal at other schools, he was the perfect person to open the school.

When Hillgrove opened in 2006, we did so with ninth to eleventh graders only. Those students came from more than twelve different middle and high schools. It was a mixture of students who were rezoned from the school they would have gone to before we opened, employees' children who came with their parents, and school-choice students who were looking for a fresh start or a new place. It had the potential to be a complete nightmare with that many cultures coming together under one roof. Joe Boland was the leader who brought us all together.

The first thing that Mr. Boland did to get everyone's attention was to be 100 percent authentic with everyone. He spoke the truth in a transparent way none of us were used to. On the first day of school, at 8:30 a.m., he got on the announcements: "Good morning, Hawks. In case you hoped you might be the first person to get in a fight at Hillgrove High School. It's too late. If you thought, 'I'll be the first person kicked out of this school'. It's too late. I hope the rest of y'all have a great first day of school." I remember starting my first class with the students there thinking, "This guy doesn't mess around." He was tough!

Joe Boland held students accountable. He insisted on the maximum discipline for fighting at school: ten days of out-of-school suspension. And while that may seem harsh, it sent a message to everyone. This is a place of learning, and if you're not here to learn, you can take two weeks off to figure it out. I'll be honest. In sixteen years at Hillgrove, I never witnessed a single fight. Did they happen? I'm sure. But not frequently enough for me to ever see one.

He also held teachers accountable. I remember talking with our football and basketball coaches about this. They both asked if we had "gotten the talk" from Mr. Boland yet. When I pressed them, they both said they had been called into his office to hear about areas for improvement. For football and basketball, Mr. Boland told them he didn't like to see their players walking around the halls with their hoods up and headphones on, not paying attention to what's going on. He told those coaches he expected them to fix it, and he trusted them to do so.

Then I got the call to come to his office. Our marching band practice field was as far away from our classroom as possible, on the other side of the building, and then another 100 yards away. At first, our students would go through the building with their equipment and personal items to get there. It was, in their defense, the shortest route. Mr. Boland wasn't having it. He wanted us to go out and around and explained that he didn't like the students walking through the building when the custodians were trying to clean it up after school. It made perfect sense to me, and we changed our policy. He never said anything else about it. He wanted us to know that we were free to lead!

But Joe Boland wasn't just tough. He was also tender.

As a leader, he was fantastic at connecting with the students and staff. He'd get on the announcements and talk about how great sports teams were doing. He would be seen in the hallway joking with students, building them up. He would talk about prom and homecoming dance, reminding the students with a smile that there would be "no nasty dancing."

He would visit classrooms and ask teachers if they needed anything, and then he would go to the bookkeeper and have her buy what they needed. He bought countless instruments for our band program, and after they were delivered, he would come down and ask, "Mr. Erwin, is the instrument that student is playing one I bought?" And when the answer was inevitably yes, he just smiled and watched. He loved students and teachers alike.

The students formed a club called "Boland's Buddies" and would sit together at football games, basketball games, and pep rallies, and cheer for him when he walked by. They cheered for the principal as much as they cheered for the team! This leader understood what it took to set up a culture where everyone felt seen, heard, and valued. He also modeled the culture and values that he wanted to see in his school.

The results? Respect! Hillgrove was immediately respected for academic, athletic, and arts excellence. We were set up to succeed by a leader who had very high standards but also a keen way of connecting with the people he led. Our teams made the playoffs every year. Our arts programs were among the best in the country, showcasing their talents on the state, national, and even international levels. Our school was consistently ranked in the top five in a district of sixteen high schools for graduation rate and test scores. I once heard a neighboring school principal ask Mr. Boland, "Is there anything your school doesn't do well?" He just smirked. He knew the answer was no.

The chief reason that we had so few behavior issues, so few retention issues (there are still teachers at the school that were there on day one), and so much excellence was the culture that Joe Boland set for the staff and the students. I can truly say that I Loved That Place then and still love it today!

IT'S YOUR TURN

I challenge you to become a tough and tender leader like Mr. Boland, a leader who embraces the sensitivity and strength that people need in today's schools. Tough and tender leaders are respected by the people they lead. That respect comes from leading with equal parts empathy and accountability. Embrace the people you lead as human beings. Listen to them. Care for them. Connect with them. Then, be there to help them grow. Leave no one behind but leave no one where you find them. Remember, compassion is a two-sided coin: empathy is on one side and accountability is on the other.

I challenge you to remember that **Good Things Come to Leaders Who HUSTLE**. To become that tough and tender leader is to embrace:

Humility
Understanding
Scholarship
Trust
Leadership
Excellence

A humble leader turns their back to the crowd. You may do more work than anyone in your building, but the credit must be shared. Being humble draws people in and convinces them to permit you to lead them. Never lose your confidence in your skills. You can do a great job and still empower others. That's what humble leaders do.

An **understanding** leader **embraces diversity as an advantage**, remembering that any friction created by diverse teams is worth the better quality of outcomes you will receive. They also **discover the unique strengths** in themselves and those they lead to empower people to use them to make the team better. No leader should try to do everything themselves. Delegating tasks to others to match their strengths is a great way to build influence.

A leader who is a **scholar** of the craft understands the power of doing a good job and the influence of building **self-discipline and focus**. Remember, a leader who is unavailable and inaccessible to team members is of no value to the team.

A **trustworthy** leader remembers the power of **gratitude and growth**. They make deposits in emotional bank accounts. Remember, a 5:1 positive-to-negative ratio of interactions is ideal when building trust.

A leader who displays good **leadership habits and attitudes** is able to color their world with the behaviors they want to see in others. Your habits will determine your future. Your attitude will determine who joins you there. Choose colors that others will want to follow.

A leader who understands that **excellence** is **more than achievement** is on their way to creating a great culture. Creating an environment where excellence is encouraged and expected starts with modeling commitment to those we lead. Celebrating those behaviors that transcend GPA and test scores is essential to helping others see themselves as valuable.

When Mr. Boland retired in 2010, we petitioned the district office to name our auditorium after him. Imagine a former football coach being honored for his contribution to the arts programs. I can tell you that every time I walked past the sign that read, "Joseph B. Boland Theater," I would say to myself, "I Love This Place." It was a feeling I would get because of the culture that a tough and tender leader helped to create.

Culture and leadership are an investment for sure. They are an investment that will take time, energy, and money. However, that investment will pay enormous dividends when the people you lead feel valued, seen, heard, and empowered to act in their school and community. Find a tool that works and set aside the time for training. And when you do this, I have no doubt everyone around you will shout from the rooftops:

I Love This Place!

THE 1-4-3 – CHAPTER 13: IT'S NOT ABOUT US

1 Quotable Quote

"Amplification happens when people know they are free to lead."

Culture doesn't multiply because of control—it multiplies because of trust. The more you release leadership, the more the culture expands.

4 Key Takeaways

1. **Your leadership ceiling becomes your culture's ceiling:** If everything flows through you, nothing grows beyond you. Great leaders create room for others to step up and lead.
2. **People need permission and space to lead:** We say we want more leaders—but often we micromanage, over-direct, or fail to invite. Culture changes when leadership becomes shared.
3. **Giving others a voice isn't a trend—it's a leadership model:** When people feel empowered to lead, they stop asking for permission to make things better. They start owning the culture.
4. **Humility unlocks amplification:** Sometimes the best thing a leader can do is get out of the way. Great

leadership isn't about always having the answers—it's about building others who will.

3 Questions for Your Team

1. How can you help others say, "I love this place," this year?
2. How can we create more opportunities for leadership?
3. What legacy do we want to leave long after we are gone?

Acknowledgments

THE UNTOLD PART of the story is that "I Love This Place" was born on a counselor's couch, in the middle of a marital crisis. It was a period where we were fighting for our lives, our relationship, our kids, everything. When my wife told me I was "talking the talk and not walking the walk," she meant it. I was a leader in name only, and it was not only impacting my home life but also my school life. The ideas in this book were born in the middle of that struggle.

What saved us? I was led to meet the greatest leader who has ever lived, and His name is Jesus. I want to first thank my Creator for being there for me, modeling great leadership for us all, and bringing so many opportunities my way to share this with others.

To Aaren and our boys, William and Andrew. I Love OUR place! It hasn't always been easy, but leading you as husband and dad has been the thrill of a lifetime. Thank you for sticking by my side in this new adventure and always encouraging me to be better and do better.

Our team, Growing Leaders, and Maxwell Leadership are the greatest I could ask for.

Thank you to Andrew McPeak for shepherding me through this process.

Dr. Tim Elmore, for being a guide, a mentor, a friend, and a fellow lover of the "dad joke."

Kara Mallory and Molly McWilliams for being such great teammates during our time working together.

Greg Steely, Jared Cagle, and Mark Cole for believing in me and helping make this all possible.

Matt Litton, the greatest content editor in the world.

And finally, to the great school leaders who helped shape my life and career up to this point: Robin Harry and Chris Ferrell for giving me a shot at my teaching dreams.

Dr. David Doke for being my travel buddy, disc golf partner, and dear friend.

Mr. Joe Boland, Dr. Robert Shaw, Mr. Christian Suttle, Mrs. Angela Stewart, Coach Ed Morris, Mrs. Amber Lamb, and Ms. Sherri Thoroughman for modeling what it means to be a great school leader.

Endnotes

Chapter 2

[1] Pulver, Clint. I Love It Here. Shadow Mountain, 2021.
[2] Fullan, Michael. The New Meaning of Educational Change. Routledge, 2007.
[3] "Our Teacher Satisfaction Survey Spanned Generations." SchoolCEO, https://www.schoolceo.com/a/our-teacher-satisfaction-survey-spanned-generations/. Accessed 1 May 2024.
[4] "Our Teacher Satisfaction Survey Spanned Generations." SchoolCEO, https://www.schoolceo.com/a/our-teacher-satisfaction-survey-spanned-generations/. Accessed 1 May 2024.
[5] ibid.
[6] ibid.
[7] *Gruenert, S., & Whitaker, T. (2015). School culture rewired: how to define, assess, and transform it. Alexandria, Virginia USA: ASCD.*
[8] "2022 Teacher Survey: Current Challenges in Teaching." AdoptAClassroom.org, https://www.adoptaclassroom.org/2022/08/01/2022-teacher-survey-current-challenges-in-teaching/. Accessed 1 May 2024.
[9] "2022 Teacher Survey: Current Challenges in Teaching." AdoptAClassroom.org, https://www.adoptaclassroom.org/2022/08/01/2022-teacher-survey-current-challenges-in-teaching/. Accessed 1 May 2024.
[10] Elmore, T. (2014). *12 huge mistakes parents can avoid: Leading your kids to succeed in life.* Harvest House Publishers.
[11] Jackson, Glen. *Preeminence.* Looking Glass Books, 2018.
[12] Elmore, Tim. *Habitudes for Communicators.* Growing Leaders, 2016.

Chapter 3

[13] Elmore, Tim. "Six Ideas to Unite Five Generations at Work." LinkedIn, https://www.linkedin.com/pulse/six-ideas-unite-five-generations-work-tim-elmore/. Accessed 1 May 2024.

Chapter 4

[14] "Quiet Confidence." Ben Meer Newsletter, https://benmeer.com/newsletter/quiet-confidence/. Accessed 1 May 2024.
[15] "David Frost, renowned journalist and TV host, dies at 74." CNN, 5 January 2009, https://www.cnn.com/2009/SHOWBIZ/Movies/01/05/david.frost/index.html. Accessed 1 May 2024.
[16] Kennedy Highest Rated Modern President, Nixon Lowest. Gallup, https://news.gallup.com/poll/145064/kennedy-highest-rated-modern-president-nixon-lowest.aspx. Accessed 1 May 2024.
[17] "The President's News Conference." The American Presidency Project, https://www.presidency.ucsb.edu/documents/the-presidents-news-conference-213. Accessed 1 May 2024.
[18] Kennedy Highest Rated Modern President, Nixon Lowest. Gallup, https://news.gallup.com/poll/145064/kennedy-highest-rated-modern-president-nixon-lowest.aspx. Accessed 1 May 2024.
[19] @AdamMGrant. ""Every[one] should learn that humility and kindness aren't signs of weakness. They're strengths of character. Recognizing your faults doesn't mean you lack self-esteem. It shows you have self-awareness. Showing compassion doesn't mean you lack backbone. It shows you have heart."" Twitter, 1 April 2023, 8:45 AM, https://twitter.com/AdamMGrant/status/12345678901234567 89.

Chapter 5

[20] Elmore, Tim. Eight Paradoxes of Great Leadership. Growing Leaders, 2016.
[21] "Chiefs' Jerick McKinnon Says Wasn't a Hesitation to Score Instead of Sliding Down in Super Bowl." MSN, https://www.msn.com/en-us/sports/nfl/chiefs-jerick-mckinnon-says-wasnt-a-hesitation-to-score-instead-of-sliding-down-in-super-bowl/ar-AA17GWqp. Accessed 1 May 2024.

Chapter 6

[22] „Gustav Mahler Symphony." GustavMahler.com, https://gustavmahler.com/symphony.html. Accessed 1 May 2024.
[23] "Infographic: Diversity & Inclusion = Better Decision Making at Work." Cloverpop Blog, https://www.cloverpop.com/blog/infographic-diversity-inclusion-better-decision-making-at-work#:~:text=Diversity%20can%20increase%20friction%2015,what%20a%20diverse%20group%20executes. Accessed 1 May 2024.

[24] "Power of Teamwork: Diverse Teams Drive Stronger Growth." The Diversity Movement, https://thediversitymovement.com/power-of-teamwork-diverse-teams-drive-stronger-growth/. Accessed 1 May 2024.
[25] ibid.
[26] "Diversity and Inclusion Revolution." Deloitte, https://www2.deloitte.com/content/dam/insights/us/articles/4209_Diversity-and-inclusion-revolution/DI_Diversity-and-inclusion-revolution.pdf. Accessed 1 May 2024.
[27] "New Surgeon General Advisory Raises Alarm About Devastating Impact of Epidemic of Loneliness and Isolation in the United States." U.S. Department of Health & Human Services, 3 May 2023, https://www.hhs.gov/about/news/2023/05/03/new-surgeon-general-advisory-raises-alarm-about-devastating-impact-epidemic-loneliness-isolation-united-states.html. Accessed 1 May 2024.
[28] "Loneliness is rising, younger workers and social media users feel it most." CNBC, 23 January 2020, https://www.cnbc.com/2020/01/23/loneliness-is-rising-younger-workers-and-social-media-users-feel-it-most.html#:~:text=The%20numbers%20remain%20even%20higher,-from%2069%25%20a%20year%20ago. Accessed 1 May 2024.
[29] Maxwell, John C. Developing the Leaders Around You. Thomas Nelson, 1995.
[30] Hanel, Paul H. P., Guillaume R. Maio, and Antony S. R. Manstead. "A New Way to Look at the Data: Similarities Between Groups of People Are Large and Important." Journal of Personality and Social Psychology, vol. 116, no. 4, 2019, pp. 541–562. doi:10.1037/pspi0000154.
*There's a wonderful graphic version of this information at https://informationisbeautiful.net/beautifulnews/781-far-more-unites-us/
[31] "Strengths-based development." Gallup, https://www.gallup.com/cliftonstrengths/en/511253/strengths-based-development.aspx#:~:text=Strengths%2Dbased%20development%20helps%20your,their%20manager%20was%20extremely%20meaningful. Accessed 1 May 2024.
[32] "Why Leaders Should Focus on Strengths, Not Weaknesses." Forbes, 6 February 2020, https://www.forbes.com/sites/forbescoachescouncil/2020/02/06/why-leaders-should-focus-on-strengths-not-weaknesses/?sh=f3678f53d1ae. Accessed 1 May 2024.
[33] "Erich Brenn: Plate Spinner." Ed Sullivan Show, https://www.edsullivan.com/artists/erich-brenn-plate-spinner/. Accessed 1 May 2024.
[34] Clear, J. (2018). *Atomic habits: An easy & proven way to build good habits & break bad ones*. Avery.

"If you can get 1% better each day for one year, you'll end up thirty-seven times better by the time you're done." (p. 15)

[35] "Clear is Kind. Unclear is Unkind." Brené Brown, https://brenebrown.com/articles/2018/10/15/clear-is-kind-unclear-is-unkind/. Accessed 1 May 2024.

[36] "It's What You Learn After You Know It All That Counts." The Wooden Effect, https://www.thewoodeneffect.com/its-what-you-learn-after-you-know-it-all-that-counts/. Accessed 1 May 2024.

[37] "Comparison of the Amundsen and Scott expeditions." Wikipedia, https://en.wikipedia.org/wiki/Comparison_of_the_Amundsen_and_Scott_expeditions#:~:text=Amundsen's%20team%20had%20plenty%20of,in%20man%2Dhauling%20the%20sledges. Accessed 1 May 2024.

[38] "What the Race to the South Pole Can Teach You About How to Achieve Your Goals." The Art of Manliness, https://www.artofmanliness.com/character/manly-lessons/what-the-race-to-the-south-pole-can-teach-you-about-how-to-achieve-your-goals/. Accessed 1 May 2024.

[39] "What the Race to the South Pole Can Teach You About How to Achieve Your Goals." The Art of Manliness, https://www.artofmanliness.com/character/manly-lessons/what-the-race-to-the-south-pole-can-teach-you-about-how-to-achieve-your-goals/. Accessed 1 May 2024.

[40] "The Magic Relationship Ratio, According to Science." Gottman Institute, https://www.gottman.com/blog/the-magic-relationship-ratio-according-science/. Accessed 1 May 2024.

[41] "Better Pay, Benefits Loom Large in Job Satisfaction." Society for Human Resource Management (SHRM), https://www.shrm.org/topics-tools/news/benefits-compensation/better-pay-benefits-loom-large-job-satisfaction#:~:text=Tellingly%2C%2094%20percent%20of%20employees,progressively%20declined%20as%20recognition%20decreased. Accessed 1 May 2024.

[42] "Challenge Coins Today and Origin Story." Police Badge and Patch, https://www.policebadgeandpatch.com/post/challenge-coins-today-and-origin-story-1. Accessed 1 May 2024.

[43] Rubin, Rick. *The Creative Act: A Way of Being*. Penguin Press. 2023

[44] ibid.

[45] "All Our Life Is But a Mass of Habits." Bensonian, https://bensonian.wordpress.com/2012/04/18/all-our-life-is-but-a-mass-of-habits/. Accessed 1 May 2024.

[46] Klein, Allen. *You Can't Ruin My Day*. Viva Editions. 2015.

[47] "Author Talks: Somebody Tell a Joke." McKinsey & Company, https://www.mckinsey.com/featured-insights/mckinsey-on-books/

author-talks-somebody-tell-a-joke?cid=other-eml-mtg-mip-mck-&hlkid=c53ee660c6ed4be588dc355410e2df35&hctky=12944766&hdpid=18c5eb77-80bb-470e-94c3-5795a6e50763. Accessed 1 May 2024.

[48] "A Healthy Attitude is Contagious, but Don't Wait to Catch It from Others; Be a Carrier." National Network of Libraries of Medicine (NNLM), https://news.nnlm.gov/region_5/a-healthy-attitude-is-contagious-but-dont-wait-to-catch-it-from-others-be-a-carrier-tom-stoppard/#:~:-text=15-,%E2%80%9CA%20healthy%20attitude%20is%20contagious%2C%20but%20don't%20wait,a%20carrier.%E2%80%9D%20%E2%80%93%20Tom%20Stoppard&text=Let's%20be%20carriers%20and%20create,spines%20that%20can%20inspire%20others. Accessed 1 May 2024.

[49] "Mehrabian's Communication Model." MindTools, https://www.mindtools.com/ao9kek8/mehrabians-communication-model. Accessed 1 May 2024.

[50] "Braving the Wilderness Excerpt." Brené Brown, https://brenebrown.com/articles/2017/09/07/braving-the-wilderness-excerpt/. Accessed 1 May 2024.

[51] Rubin, Rick. *The Creative Act: A Way of Being*. Penguin Press. 2023. (Adapted)

[52] Gopnik, Adam. *The Real Work*. Liveright Publishing. 2023.

[53] ibid.

[54] Story adapted from Gopnik, Adam. *The Real Work*. Liveright Publishing. 2023.

[55] "2022 Teacher Survey: Current Challenges in Teaching." AdoptAClassroom.org, https://www.adoptaclassroom.org/2022/08/01/2022-teacher-survey-current-challenges-in-teaching/. Accessed 1 May 2024.

[56] "Understanding the Social Ripple Effect." Social Impact Architects, https://socialimpactarchitects.com/social-ripple-effect/. Accessed 1 May 2024.

[57] "Forget Likes: What the World Needs Now Is Love." AJC, https://www.ajc.com/lifestyles/forget-likes-what-the-world-needs-now-love/F8dmkJFRQOW5eZuKavxshK/. Accessed 1 May 2024.

[58] "What Is Company Culture?" BambooHR, https://www.bamboohr.com/blog/what-is-company-culture. Accessed 1 May 2024.

www.ingramcontent.com/pod-product-compliance
Lightning Source LLC
LaVergne TN
LVHW041928090826
845145LV00017B/2033